GunDigest

SHOOTER'S HANDGUN
GUIDE to
MARKSMANSHIP

PETER LESSLER

Published by

Gun Digest® Books, an imprint of F+W Media, Inc.
Krause Publications • 700 East State Street • Iola, WI 54990-0001
715-445-2214 • 888-457-2873
www.krausebooks.com

To order books or other products call toll-free 1-800-258-0929
or visit us online at www.gundigeststore.com

Featuring photos by Richard Gugeler of Ragtop Photography

ISBN-13: 978-1-4402-3606-8
ISBN-10: 1-4402-3606-2

Edited by Jennifer L.S. Pearsall
Cover Design by Al West
Designed by Nicole MacMartin

Printed in USA

10 9 8 7 6 5 4 3

CONTENTS

INTRODUCTION

This book is not about handguns. Nor is it about holsters, or concealed carry, or fighting tactics, or winning practical shooting matches. There are many good books, DVDs, and schools on such subjects, and I encourage you investigate them. This book is, instead, about three concepts. First, it's about how to think about keeping yourself aware, safe, and ready in environments where self-defense with a handgun may be necessary. Second, it's also about learning to shoot a pistol with consistent sufficient accuracy, recoil control, and the learned physical and mental reflexes that allow the development of the high-speed application of that accuracy. Finally, it's about learning all the necessary handling techniques to support fast and accurate shooting: safe gun handling, the draw from a belt holster, reloading, and clearing malfunctions under stress. These are the foundational skills that form a complete skill set and allow progression to a high performance level. They will serve you equally well in a self-defense encounter or in shooting a practical competition event simulating such situations. (Why the aspect of competition? Because a mid-level competitive practical shooter is probably at the ninety-fifth or higher percentile skill level compared to all other handgun owners, including the "government employee" types.) This book will help you get there.

The method of properly using a large-caliber pistol for the purpose of self-defense underwent a major advance in the latter half of the twentieth

> ## "Good shooting is good execution of the fundamentals. Great shooting is great execution of the fundamentals"
> —Jim Starr, coach of the Colorado junior high power rifle team, quoting a champion shooter.

century. Led by former Marine Lt. Col. Jeff Cooper and a group of his friends comprised of civilian recreational shooters, law enforcement officers, and hunters, this effort used open, freestyle competition to develop and compare ideas, equipment, and techniques against scenarios based on personal combat experiences and other actual instances of shootouts. By the end of that century, techniques allowing great advances in fast and accurate shooting had been devised, along with an understanding of how both the pistol and the human mind are best used in defensive situations. What has since been named the "Modern Technique of the Pistol" was born, it being equal parts marksmanship, gun handling, and mindset. The following section deals with these concepts, but geared to the beginner and intermediate shooter. While there is no substitute for training under with qualified coach, it is my intent to provide sufficient material here to enable a beginner to learn, understand, and practice the Modern Technique correctly and with some capacity for self-analysis when a proper coach is unavailable.

The U.S. Army method of teaching skills is the "crawl-walk-run" method. One thing at a time, learned at a basic level, then more things, then performing at more advanced levels. Trying to make people run before they have mastered walking or even crawling is usually counterproductive. I've seen a number of people in competition and training environments trying to do things far beyond their capacity and without recognizing the gaps in their abilities. Often they have no idea what they're missing, and pride and ego prevent their listening to well-intentioned suggestions. They have the expensive and fancy gear and they watched some guy on TV or a DVD, and to them, that's what matters, right?

Wrong. Without knowing all the foundational skills, your performance will suffer. Without patiently working on each skill, the boredom of high repetition and the ego-bruising of honest self-evaluation sets in and your performance will suffer. Without a solid "crawl-walk" foundation, you will never learn to "run" at the high level most of us desire.

Did you see the Jim Starr quote? "Running" usually means performing what you already know how to do at the "walk" without error, but faster. My approach in this book focuses on the "crawl-walk" part. It is the most important part and, if I can get you from "crawl" to "walk," well, you'll have all the skills necessary to progress to the "run" on your own, or with help from a local competitor who "runs" well. So read, think, and train with this in mind. Care, patience, and determination in learning the following foundation can get you to that ninety-fifth percentile faster than you think.

THE FOUR SAFETY RULES

Before we delve into the art and science of pistol marksmanship, let's look at the basic gun handling safety rules, as codified by Col. Jeff Cooper.

ALL GUNS ARE ALWAYS LOADED

This does not mean you keep all your guns loaded all the time. It means you always treat a gun as though it were loaded *even when you know it's not*. The reason for this is that some people seem to think it's okay to handle a gun less safely if they think it is unloaded, and the problem with that mindset is that they may be mistaken! "I didn't know it was loaded!" is the cry heard after an accidental (actually negligent) discharge. Know how to check if a gun is loaded or unloaded. Perform this check every time you handle a gun, and regardless what you "know" of gun's condition, always *treat* it as if loaded, *all* the time.

NEVER LET THE MUZZLE POINT AT ANYTHING YOU DO NOT WISH TO DESTROY

Keep in control of your gun's muzzle direction at all times and always keep it pointed in a safe direction. That means knowing and being aware of what and where a safe direction is. *You* are responsible every moment you have a gun in your hands.

KEEP YOUR FINGER OFF THE TRIGGER UNTIL YOUR SIGHTS ARE ON THE TARGET

The trigger fires the gun. You have no business casually placing your finger on the trigger while handling a gun in any manner other than the actual and specific act of firing. This is probably the worst habit untrained people display; their finger goes right on the trigger as soon as they pick up the gun. If you're not prepared to shoot, keep the finger straight along the outside of the trigger guard.

BE CERTAIN OF YOUR TARGET AND WHAT IS BEYOND IT

Do not fire at a sound or an unidentified shape. When practicing, make sure you have a safe backstop to halt every bullet you fire. Bullets tend to go through things, so, even if you hit your target, the bullet can keep going. A miss keeps going, too. Make sure you control where every bullet stops. A bullet has no friends once it leaves the gun muzzle, and you can't stop it or turn it back.

These rules must be adhered to *at all times* when handling guns, either on the range, at home, in a gun store or gun show, etc. *There are no exceptions!* Lives are at stake. Keep your wits about you and your mind on what you're doing whenever you handle a firearm. If you can't do two things at once, put the gun down, attend to whatever is distracting you, and then resume the gun business. These four rules *must* become second nature if you are to have anything to do with firearms. *You* are responsible every second you have a gun in your hands.

CHAPTER 1
MINDSET

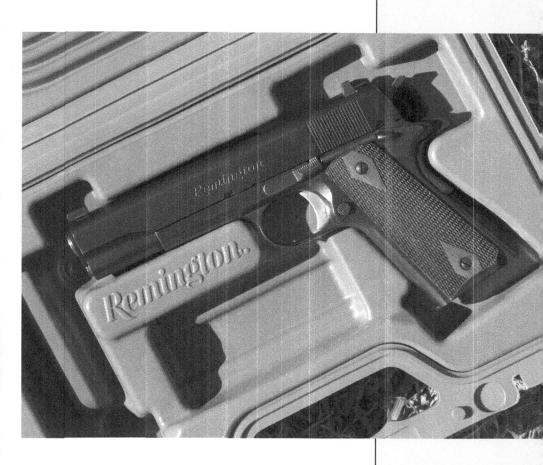

K eep in mind that all of the following dissertation is designed to enable you to do three things: get your pistol
into action quickly, place a shot or shots with sufficient
speed and accuracy to solve the problem you are facing, and
keep your gun running through any mechanical difficulties.
Accomplishing these things requires more than raw physical skills. It also requires a mental clarity and composure that

*The classic 1911A1 .45
Automatic Government
Model, this example by
Remington Arms.*

keeps a mind under stress from interfering with your shooting mechanics and allows maximum physical performance based on highly ingrained physical skills that have become subconscious reflexes. This allows the higher conscious mind to concentrate on other problem solving considerations, such as tactics, finding an escape route, etc. To achieve clarity and composure while shooting, we need to work on them during practice sessions, and also while attending shooting matches from time to time, so as to learn to deal with the extra stresses competition creates. Further benefits of competition are the opportunities to witness some highly skilled performances, to learn from those shooters, and to accurately gauge where your own performance stands in comparison.

We also need mental preparation, though, of a different sort, in advance of any real-life crisis. Having to face a deadly, real-world criminal attack without being mentally prepared to some degree can be a recipe for disaster; we may find it impossible to get our mental feet under us in time to react quickly enough to save the day. Since we don't know when a crisis may pop up, we really need to be prepared for the worst on a daily basis from the time we get out of bed every morning. We must develop a daily mindset in which the sudden appearance of a couple armed hoodlums not only does not flummox us, but instead activates a pre-planned sequence of well-practiced actions that result in our standing over their prostrate bodies with a smoking pistol in our hands.

If that idea, that vision, is somewhat shocking to certain readers—"My God, I really don't want to *actually shoot someone!*"—let me ask you, would you rather it was you on the ground in a pool of blood, with the hoodlums ransacking your pockets? I also have to ask, do you actually carry a gun with you every day or have one in the house for self-defense? If you do (which is why you are reading this), then you have to really and honestly face

A full-size Government Model 1911A1 .45 shown with the Springfield Compact Model 1911, which is shorter in both barrel length and grip frame length.

Left to right: .45 ACP 230-grain full metal jacket, .45 ACP hollowpoint, and .45 ACP lead semi-wadcutter.

Left to right: .45 ACP full metal jacket ("ball") and .40 Smith & Wesson flat point.

From left to right: The .380 Auto holllowpoint, 9x19mm Luger, .45 ACP ball, .32 ACP, and .22 Long Rifle rimfire.

the fact that every time you get up in the morning (or go to sleep at night), you just might have to use the thing. While it is true that many (some say most) confrontations are ended by the mere sight of the defender's gun, there are always exceptions. Heck, I don't want to shoot anybody any more than anyone else does. I just want to make it home every day in one piece.

When considering these matters, treat the development of your mindset with the life-saving seriousness it deserves. Understand that, while the pistol section of this book may deal with technical matters of marksmanship and gun handling techniques, the purpose of these skills is to save your life in a potentially lethal fight. Being a mere technician with a gun is not enough; a number of good pistol marksmen have come out on the wrong end of deadly encounters, simply because their mindset was wrong. If you ever have to use your pistol in self-defense, it will generally not require very high marksmanship skills. However, if you wish to survive and win, it will require you to have the right mindset. You must develop a "combat mindset," one that prepares you to go from ordinary peaceful citizen to aware, skilled, and determined fighter in a heartbeat. Without this mental ability, you may not survive a sudden and unexpected assault, nor may you be able press the trigger while

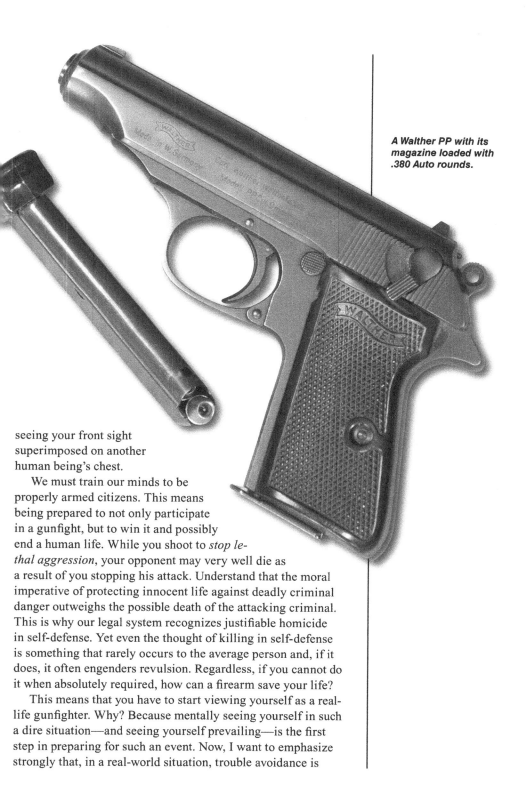

A Walther PP with its magazine loaded with .380 Auto rounds.

seeing your front sight superimposed on another human being's chest.

We must train our minds to be properly armed citizens. This means being prepared to not only participate in a gunfight, but to win it and possibly end a human life. While you shoot to *stop lethal aggression*, your opponent may very well die as a result of you stopping his attack. Understand that the moral imperative of protecting innocent life against deadly criminal danger outweighs the possible death of the attacking criminal. This is why our legal system recognizes justifiable homicide in self-defense. Yet even the thought of killing in self-defense is something that rarely occurs to the average person and, if it does, it often engenders revulsion. Regardless, if you cannot do it when absolutely required, how can a firearm save your life?

This means that you have to start viewing yourself as a real-life gunfighter. Why? Because mentally seeing yourself in such a dire situation—and seeing yourself prevailing—is the first step in preparing for such an event. Now, I want to emphasize strongly that, in a real-world situation, trouble avoidance is

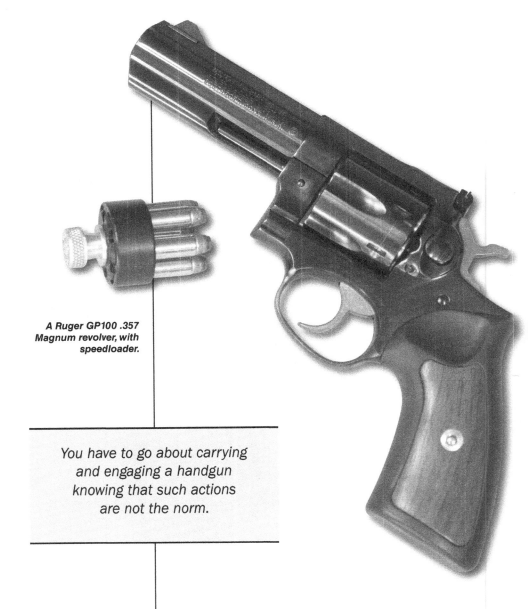

A Ruger GP100 .357 Magnum revolver, with speedloader.

You have to go about carrying and engaging a handgun knowing that such actions are not the norm.

always your first priority, de-escalation your second, and escape your third. Pulling your gun is only for when you are in reasonable fear of your life and there is absolutely no other action open to you besides dying. Remember, after you solve problem one (the attack) you'll still have problem two (the trial), where you will have to show the court and jury that your actions were reasonable under the circumstances.

Circling back to a dire situation, you have to go about the business of carrying and engaging a handgun knowing that such actions are not the norm. All of us have a built-in hesitancy to harm another person, even when such harm is clearly necessary

From left to right: .357 Magnum, .45 ACP ball, .44 Magnum.

and justifiable in the moral and legal senses. But hesitancy in a justified situation can get us killed. We have to take steps to overcome certain natural obstacles such as this with a mental preparation program.

The biggest mental blocks to being fully capable of winning a gunfight are paralyzing fear or surprise and the normal reluctance of a civilized person to severely injure or kill a fellow human being. Colonel Jeff Cooper, master firearms instructor and the greatest single contributor to the development of the Modern Technique of the Defensive Handgun (marksmanship, gun handling, and mindset), believes that, when it comes to winning a lethal confrontation, mindset is even more important than marksmanship. Cooper came up with a program to address these issues, one that's seen wide acceptance in recent years.

Let's tackle the fear issue first. Having never been in a gunfight, this author can only rely on the words of those who have "seen the elephant." One of the most interesting observations on courage under fire comes from the brilliant warrior leader Gen. George S. Patton, Jr., of World War II fame. He said something along the lines of, "Courage comes from confidence, and confidence comes from demonstrated ability." He also said, regarding training, "A pint of sweat saves a gallon of blood."

Hmm … . Hard training yields ability that can be demonstrated on demand, which in turn breeds self-confidence and, thus, courage in battle. What did I say earlier about lots and lots of practice? If you are a beginning shooter, you may find it difficult to envisage yourself in a real fight for your life and wielding your handgun with speed, smoothness, accuracy, and coolness. But it's not so hard when you can see those qualities beginning to develop in yourself in your practice sessions. What your target and the clock show you are what build that confidence. So practice, practice, practice. Don't let a handgun that sits in a drawer be a false security blanket. It is your demonstrable skill that gives the gun its real value. This skill has to be earned the hard way, with consistent practice—and being a perishable skill, it must be maintained the same way.

Some crises can happen so quickly that you'll barely have time to react, let alone get scared. Fear actually takes some time to build. If you find yourself in a situation where you have that time for the fear to build up but still cannot escape, Col. Cooper recommended that you attempt to twist the fear into anger. Get angry at those who are threatening you and use that anger to

From left to right: The .40 S&W, .380 Auto, .32 ACP, and .25 ACP.

Star's Model 30M in 9mm Luger, with a 15-round magazine.

fuel your own courage. Remember, if you are properly armed, properly trained and skilled, and properly oriented mentally, you are a very, very tough target and almost certainly more than a match for the average criminal. Do not think, *"Oh my God, what am I going to do? They're going to kill me!"* Instead, shake your head and think, *"I thought this might happen! Those poor fools, I'm ready for them, and they won't stand a chance."* Obviously we don't want to cross the line into overconfidence, but think about it. If you scratched a Marine or Green Beret, they'd bleed the latter remark, not the former (and they might not take kindly to being scratched, either). "But I'm no Marine!" you might say. Well, what's the difference between a soldier and

Opposite: You must
be and stay alert at all
times when carrying a
handgun. It will do you
no good to carry if you
are caught unaware in
a bad situation, as you
may not have the time
to draw, and you risk the
chance of having your
gun grabbed from you in
a face-to-face encounter.

you? Training and attitude, that's what. You can gain enough of both on your own, if you follow the right path.

THE MENTAL COLOR CODE

As for being frozen in surprise or hesitant to pull the trigger when justified and necessary, Col. Cooper devised a program that handles both of these at once. This is what's now commonly known as the "Color Code" scheme. The colors are white, yellow, orange, and red. Unlike the terrorist threat level color codes, Cooper's color code has nothing to do with danger, rather each color is tied to a specific mental state. The purpose is two-fold: to foster alertness so as not to be taken by surprise, and to

use this alertness to create enough time for a person to prepare mentally for the imminent possible application of lethal force.

Condition White is where most people spend their lives—unaware of their surroundings, lost in their own little worlds, with no thought of potential dangers. It is possible to walk right up to a person in White and bop them on the head. They'll never see it coming. Obviously, this is a poor place to be if we are concerned about our safety. If you are carrying a gun, you have no business being in White unless you are asleep. In White, you are mentally unprepared to deal quickly and decisively with a sudden and unexpected close-range deadly threat.

Condition Yellow is where you must be as a constant habit. You wake up in the morning and acknowledge that you may find yourself in danger that day. So you pay attention to your surroundings. You engage in what is, essentially, people watching. You know who is around and behind you, you note what kind of car is following you, you will notice if any person or group is staring at you or keying their actions to yours. You do not have any specific cause for alarm, nor are you being paranoid. You are simply engaging in relaxed alert observation on a constant basis.

Condition Orange is when, through your alert observations in Yellow, you detect something fishy. Someone is acting in such a way as to arouse your suspicions about their intent. The clues can be varied, but someone following you or pacing you on the other side of the street while eyeing you, or a car that follows you through several direction changes, are the most obvious giveaways. At this point, you now have a focal point for your attention. It may not be an actual threat, but it has the appearance of a potential one. You must still keep your attention cast out in all directions, just as you would in Yellow, but now you have something specific to think about, and now you must start thinking of possible responses if a threat does materialize. Look for escape routes from your current position or crowded places in which to seek shelter. Start thinking along the lines of, "If he does A, I'm going to do B." Develop a set of responses to any threatening actions you can imagine.

Now is also the time to start realizing that, if things go really badly, you may have to draw and fire your gun at that person right over there. You may have to kill him. At this point you have to come to the conclusion that, if the situation warrants it, you will use deadly force. This is where you have time to steel yourself for the ultimate act. To go from Yellow to Orange, you not only have to be observant enough to

> *If flight is impossible, then you must fight with all the speed, power, and ruthlessness you can muster. The criminal should find out he has just bitten off more than he can chew.*

spot an anomaly, you have to be honest enough with yourself to recognize it for what it is and face up to the implications. This is no place for the "Oh, it's nothing, nothing at all, really" habit of denial some people have. Orange is where you make decisions, while you are still thinking calmly, before a situation explodes in your face. This relieves you of having to do so after a situation explodes, so that, instead, you then simply activate your planned response.

Condition Red is when the potential threat becomes an actual threat—the suspicious person launches a criminal attack on you. One thing you need to do ahead of time is to train yourself to look for and respond to visual cues of lethal danger. A gun pointed at you, the sudden appearance of a knife heading your way, or something similarly unmistakable, should be ingrained in your mind as the mental trigger that sets loose your lethal force defense response. Drill this into your mind ahead of time; you do not want to be figuring this out in a situation as it is unfolding. Condition Red is achieved when you see the event that trips your mental trigger—"*Go!*" You will already have seen trouble coming, made contingency plans in your head, and prepared yourself to perform fight or flight. If flight works, great, for that's the most desirable course, from the standpoint of personal-defense

Here's something you won't normally see, a German model 1923 Parabellum (commonly called the Luger) in caliber 7.65 (.30 Luger), along with a photograph of General Franz Halder, Chief of the German General Staff, 1938-1942, inscribed to Major Russell Gugeler, U.S. Army, the photographer's father.

away from your home. But, if flight is impossible, then you must fight with all the speed, power, and ruthlessness you can muster. At this point, the criminal should find out he has just bitten off more than he can chew by walking into a human buzz saw, and your part in the conflict, if you have to shoot, should seem like just another range drill: draw, get on your front sight, and fire good hits as fast as you can until the threat is eliminated.

In his priceless 44-page booklet *Principles of Personal Defense*, Col. Cooper expounds upon what he considers to be the most important mental characteristics to display when faced with danger. They are alertness, decisiveness, aggressiveness, speed, coolness, ruthlessness, and surprise, with the rationale for each explained. It is well worth (worth your life!) perusing.

Now, isn't all this much better than being taken by surprise while wandering around oblivious in Condition White? It should be reiterated. To go from Condition White to Condition Red is too much of a leap for the average person. It can get you killed. Skipping from Yellow straight to Red is possible, but difficult. But the step by step progression is quite easy and efficient. Understanding and living by the color code requires a change of habits, which will take work and time, but, in return, it offers the means to survive and even prevail in a situation that can kill the unprepared. Live by the code or die without it. The choice is yours.

CHAPTER 2

SIGHTS AND SIGHT PICTURE

"You must first achieve with your hands, and as quickly as possible, a near-perfect sight alignment with the target, then visually acquire and judge the correctness of your sight picture. Hands first, eyes second."

Using the sights to aim the gun gives you a means of verifying where the gun is pointed. To shoot without using the sights is to engage in guesswork. While it may be possible to shoot effectively at very close range, it still takes an enormous amount of practice for your hand and arm to learn to point the gun consistently in the direction your eyes are looking (a topic I will cover later). While a shooter with extensive practice will be able to hit at close range (say, under 10 yards), with reasonable consistency, for a beginner, the time required to learn to hit consistently at short range without sights will almost certainly be far greater than the time required to simply learn to use the sights correctly and quickly to get accurate, dependable results at ranges both near and far. Any sort of precise shooting requires the use of the sights and, with practice, their use can be so fast as to render moot any time difference between sighted and unsighted fire—the upside to sights is that, with their use, accuracy can be guaranteed as long as the shooter does his part.

The two most important components of sight use are to focus the eyes on the front sight and then verify the alignment between front and rear sights. The eyes can only focus in one distance plane at one point, and the front sight, rear sight, and target will all be at different distances from the eyes. The reason we pick the front sight as our focus object is that this little stub of metal tells us where the gun is aiming.

Incorrect sight focus. Note the blurry front and rear sights versus the sharply focused target. This is a common cause of inaccurate shooting.

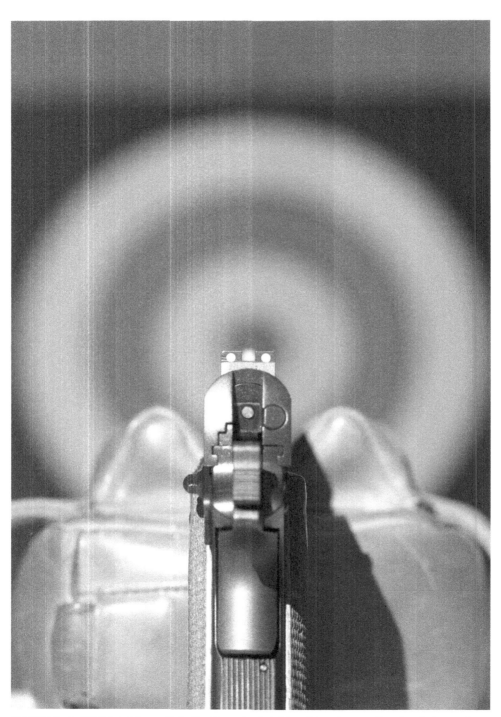

Another form of incorrect focus. Note the blurry front sight and target versus the sharply focused rear sight. This also will cause inaccurate shooting.

This is correct focus. Note the sharp front sight and blurry rear sight and target. This is what you must see for accurate shooting.

When we focus on the target, the front and rear sights will both be blurry. In this case, a small misalignment of the gun (which would be visible as sight misalignment) will not be noticed, and the gun will be looking along a different line of sight than our eyes are looking. It does not take much of an angular misalignment in the gun barrel versus our eyesight line for the shot to miss the target completely, and since this misalignment represents two diverging lines, the amount of error will grow rapidly with increasing distance to the target.

So, again, we focus on our front sight. This puts the target out of focus, just as it does the rear sights, but, in this case, it's not a drawback, since just about anything we will be shooting at with an iron-sighted pistol will be easy to see in general. Any error caused by aiming at a slightly blurry target will only be as big as the blurry edge of the target, which is actually a very small amount of space; truly, it is negligible, especially compared to the potential of the misalignment error allowed by not looking at your sights. So, we focus on the front sight and let the target blur slightly.

Coaching a young shooter how to focus on the front sights, as they relate to the rear sights and the target.

Now, how exactly do we use the sights to aim? First, we must create proper sight alignment. This is the line-up between the front and rear sights. With conventional pistol iron sights, we have a straight, square-topped post for a front sight, with a flat-topped rear sight blade that has a rectangular or square notch cut in its middle. The front sight post should be aligned in the rear sight notch so that the top flat surface of the front post is even with the top flat surface of the rear blade, and also centered side to side so that there is an even amount of space between the left side of the front post and left side of the rear notch, and the right side of the front post and right edge of the rear notch.

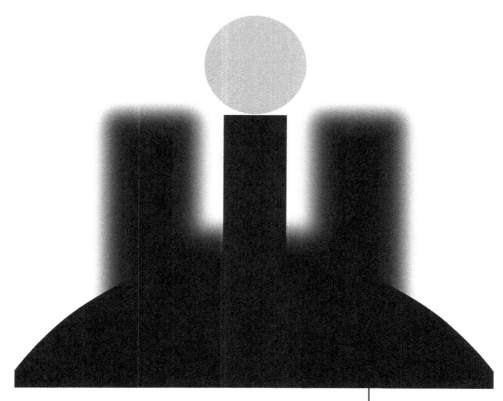

This is proper sight alignment. What your eyes should be focused on is the center of the top flat surface of the front sight post. It is this exact point that you use to place the sights on the desired impact point on the target. It is important to note that even a tiny, visible misalignment between front and rear sights actually represents a considerable angular misalignment of the gun barrel from our line of sight to the target. Thus, it is very important (especially if you are a beginner) to be a perfectionist in your sight alignment.

Proper sight alignment is achieved through your hands. As you will see later, training your hands to bring the handgun up into perfect sight alignment is one of the skills you must eventually master. This is extremely important. No one can hold a gun perfectly steady, but we must strive to eliminate error from our sight alignment. It is better to have the gun wobbling around a bit with the sights in excellent alignment with each other, than to have the gun seem steady but have the front sight off-center in the rear notch. The reason is that, if our

The six o'clock hold sight picture on a bull's-eye target. Focus on the center of the top edge of the front sight post. Let the target blur.

The center mass hold sight picture on the same bull's-eye target. Focus on the center top edge of the front post and let the target blur.

sights are aligned on a wobbling gun, our shot will hit right where the tip of the front sight happens to be aiming at the instant of discharge. As long as we can keep our "wobble zone" in an area where we would like the bullet to hit, we can fire at any point in our wobbling. On the other hand, if our sights are in misalignment at the moment of discharge, the shot will hit a considerable distance from the point where the sights are superimposed on the target, because the gun is "looking" in a different direction than our are our eyes. At close range this doesn't matter so much, but, at long ranges or on small targets, we need the most perfect alignment possible. It will be reiterated later, but get used to the notion right now of not firing a shot until you are satisfied with the sight alignment. Failure to follow this principle will result in poor accuracy.

When we move this aligned package of front and rear sights onto the target and onto the point of the target we desire

to hit (or desire to use as an aiming reference), we now have what is called a "sight picture." Proper sight alignment is what your eyes see when the front and rear sights are aligned with each other correctly, and sight picture is what your eyes see when this proper sight alignment is moved onto the target in the correct place to put the bullet where we want it.

There are two methods of aiming the sights against a target: one is "center mass," whereby you aim the top of the front sight at the very center of the object you want to hit. The other is the "edge-of-mass" hold, also commonly referred to as the "six o'clock hold." This second term stems from target shooters using round, black, bull's-eye targets. They place the top of the front sight against the bottom edge of the round black bull's-eye, so their sight picture looks like a black ball sitting on top of a black post. In this way they can clearly see the black front sight against the white of the rest of the target

The center mass sight picture on the criminal trying to kill you. Focus on the center of the top edge of the front sight post. Let the target blur.

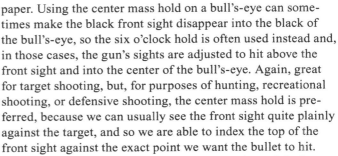

paper. Using the center mass hold on a bull's-eye can sometimes make the black front sight disappear into the black of the bull's-eye, so the six o'clock hold is often used instead and, in those cases, the gun's sights are adjusted to hit above the front sight and into the center of the bull's-eye. Again, great for target shooting, but, for purposes of hunting, recreational shooting, or defensive shooting, the center mass hold is preferred, because we can usually see the front sight quite plainly against the target, and so we are able to index the top of the front sight against the exact point we want the bullet to hit.

In practice, we often have difficulty with front sight focus, because the first thing we look at is the target—*then*, we bring the gun into our line of sight, but don't shift focus back to our front sight. This shift of eye focus from target to front sight is one of the most important concepts in proper aiming, especially when we attempt speed. Remember to shift your focus from target to sights and *always be looking at your front sight.* This is supremely important.

Speaking of speed, one goal to work towards is to first achieve with the hands a near-perfect sight alignment with the target as quickly as possible, then visually acquire and judge the correctness of your sight picture as rapidly as can be done. At this point the mind says "good to go" to a good sight picture and commences the trigger squeeze, or says "not yet" to a bad sight picture and corrects it to good one before commencing the trigger squeeze. This combines two notions. The first is the "flash sight picture," in which we recognize our sight picture and judge it in a bare instant. The second notion is that the sight picture is the boss, not the trigger finger. In other words, our sight picture

Examining a target can help demonstrate where the focus had been when the shot was broken and how the bullet then strayed from the intended path. Focus on the rear sights or the target result in an incorrect aim and hit.

is the go/no-go determinant of whether we fire the shot. No trigger pressure should be applied until our eyes have acquired the sight picture and our brain has approved it. This concept should be burned into the circuitry of your brain: *The brain controls the trigger finger based on what the eyes see.* This is the basic principle of accurate pistol shooting.

At this point, one other necessary skill becomes possible: calling your shot. Unlike billiards, where you call the pocket where you intend to sink your ball, with firearms, we see

Sight Types

There are two kinds of handgun sights, fixed and adjustable. Most semi-automatic handguns come with what are called fixed sights, and most revolvers come with what are called adjustable sights.

With adjustable sights, usually the rear sight blade can be moved from side to side and up or down by means of turning screws. This allows the sights to be more precisely aligned with the direction in which the barrel will launch the bullet. They are useful when shooting many different kinds of ammunition in the same gun (since different kinds can shoot to different points of impact), or where extremely precise shot placement at longer distances is desired, such as for target competition or hunting. When using them, remember to move the rear sight in the direction you want the shot impact to move.

The fixed-type rear sight may offer merely a groove in the top of a revolver frame, or it can be a rear blade in a dovetail groove in the slide of an semi-automatic that may be drifted slightly from side to side to fine-tune the impact point right or left. The front sights on almost all guns are totally non-adjustable, though, if the gun shoots very low, they may be filed down a little to raise up the point of impact. The majority of fixed sights are very well regulated at the factory to shoot most common types of ammunition very close to your point of aim—certainly close enough for defensive work—so try not to blame your sights if you are having troubles!

Targets

For simply learning to hit what you are aiming at, almost any kind of target will do, as long as there is a specific spot at which to aim and that spot allows you to clearly see your front sight in contrast against it. For learning precision, use a smaller aiming point of a few inches rather than simply trying to hold center mass on a large, uniform-looking surface (be thinking "aim small, miss small"). At some point, however, you'll want to change over to a humanoid-form target and practice hits in the upper chest area to train your mind in what to see and do.

An IPSC competition cardboard target. You can see the different scoring areas, including those for "head"-zone hits.

where the sights are pointing at the instant of discharge, and this tells us where the shot has gone. If the gun wavered just a bit at that instant, we will see it and know where our shot should have impacted. Calling your shot helps you shoot more accurately in that you will know where every shot has landed without having to look at the target, and you will know that it was your motion of the gun rather than some other factor that was responsible.

One more detail to talk about is follow-through. Many people fire a shot and then immediately lower the gun to look at the target. Do *not* do this! Instead, keep your eyes on your sights, even as the gun is recoiling. Train yourself to see the full recoil cycle of the gun and its return to rest. If you are doing everything right, it will return to the exact same sight picture you had the instant before the gun fired. Work on maintaining front sight focus so that you see this sight picture recovery. You will not need to see the target to ascertain your hit, because by seeing your sight picture at the instant of discharge, you will already know where the shot went. Stay on your sights! This habit is what allows you to develop speed for successive hits and is very important.

CHAPTER 3

PROPER MANAGEMENT OF THE TRIGGER

I f there is one act in the simple process of firing a shot that causes us the most trouble, it will be the pressing of the trigger. Think about that. One merely has to view the gun's sights and verify proper alignment, press the trigger to discharge the piece, and the shot will go right where the gun

The strong-hand grip with the barrel and forearm aligned properly.

is aimed. Simple as could be, right? Unfortunately, we humans tend to often make simple things complicated.

How do we avoid ruining a shot? First, let's take a look at what we need to do correctly, then we'll view what we do to foul up ourselves.

THE TRIGGER PULL

The first thing to consider is the physical aspect of the trigger pull. Pressing the trigger results in an energy input into the gun. For instance, a pistol weighing two or 2½ pounds, may have a trigger pull anywhere from its own weight (say, the pull on a cocked Smith and Wesson revolver), on up to around 14 pounds (the double-action hammer-cocking pull on some semi-autos and revolvers). Obviously, exerting 12 or 14 pounds of trigger pull pressure on a two-pound pistol creates some issues, in terms of disrupting the ability to aim steadily.

Exerting 12 or 14 pounds of trigger pull pressure on a two-pound pistol creates some issues, in terms of disrupting the ability to aim steadily.

First, let's consider firing a shot from a pistol with its hammer cocked, which requires no more than, say, 4½ pounds of finger pressure. How can we press the trigger with more force than the gun weighs, without causing the gun to move? The key here is to hold the pistol in the hand in such a way that our trigger finger sits comfortably on the trigger and can pull it straight to the rear, the same direction the mechanical motion of the trigger requires. In this action, we want to minimize any horizontal or vertical motions that may be imparted to the gun. The way to do this is to first grip the pistol so that its backstrap (the rear face of the grip frame) is centered in the web of the shooting hand between thumb and forefinger. The result of this is to align the barrel naturally with the long bones of the forearm.

Grip the gun as just described, with one hand only, and look down at your forearm and the gun. The barrel should not point to either side of a line running down the center of your forearm. (Realize that, when we progress to describing the two-handed grip, that will involve some bending of the wrists and the gun will no longer be aligned with the forearm bones in the shooting stance. This is okay, as long as the grip on the gun with the strong hand is correct as just described. Once the wrist bends in the two-handed stance, it will not affect the correct grip you have achieved on the gun.) This is the best grip with which to allow your trigger finger to pull straight to the rear without inadvertently pulling or pushing the gun to one side or another.

Next, try to place the center of the pad of the end of the finger on the trigger, rather than the very tip or the crease of the last joint. It is worth noting that the length of the finger versus the length of reach to the trigger may cause some variance here.

Hold the pistol as high up on the grip as you can. For a revolver, the top of the hand should be about even with the top of the stock. For semi-autos, cram your hand as far up against the rear tang of the grip as it will go; no space should appear between the top of your hand and the bottom of the tang. This helps mitigate muzzle jump during recoil, due to your hand being closer to the axis of that recoil (which is along the barrel).

Once you've established the correct alignment in your grip, relax the grip of the gun hand. Beginners often death-grip the pistol. But a tight gun hand prevents the trigger finger from moving rapidly, which keeps us from being able to gain speed in our shooting. In reality, you should have no more tension in your gun grip than that used when having a slightly firm handshake with a woman. The bone-crushing John Wayne grip is a no-no. The reason for this is that, when your hand is that tight, it becomes difficult, if not impossible, to allow the trigger finger to flex independently from the rest of the hand.

This independent operation is crucial. Without it, the entire hand has a tendency to squeeze when pulling the trigger, which will move the gun a considerable amount; for a right-hander, this will often result in a shot low and to the left of the aiming point (the opposite, of course, for a left-handed shooter). We want to eliminate all motion of the gun while pulling the trigger, and the gripping techniques described here, including the gentle, non-violent pressure straight rearwards as applied by the fingertip, are the methods that best accomplish this.

MINDSET AND THE SURPRISE BREAK

The action of the mind has the greatest effect of all. Ideally, you want a relaxed, calm, and empty mind when firing the shot. The only thought you should have is one of admiration for your sight picture. It is preferable to have no conscious thought of the act of pressing the trigger, or of wishing or expecting the shot to fire. If you believe that your only job is to aim, and that someone else will pull the trigger for you, you'll be on the right track.

Why this kind of "disembodied" mindset? Because the three greatest impediments to firing a clean shot are the push of the hand against the gun in anticipation of recoil as the trigger press starts; a perceived need to force the shot, when a wobbling gun presents a perfect sight picture for an instant; or an impatient desire to force the shot, even if the sight picture is incorrect. The emotional baggage we bring to the act of shooting—fear, nervousness, excitement, ego, pride, impatience, etc.—clutter our ability to perform the simplest physical act of moving our fingertip a sixteenth of an inch. It is imperative you learn to empty your mind of any thought or emotion beyond simply focusing on your sight picture.

FLINCHING

The single greatest impediment to fast and accurate shooting, in my opinion, is the anticipation of and premature reaction to recoil. This is known as a "flinching." This happens when, as soon as we press on the trigger to discharge the shot, our subconscious mind, anticipating the recoil to come, starts our hand dipping downward to counteract it. Our subconscious knows that the recoil impulse arrives pursuant to the press of the finger. The result is that the shot goes low. If the whole hand clenches convulsively at the same time, the shot will often go to the side, as well, usually left for a right-hander.

Further complicating the problem, since the flinch reflex almost always includes an eye blink, we do not see our sights dipping in the instance before the shot fires. This is probably the biggest problem encountered by people shooting a centerfire pistol with any appreciable recoil, and it is a difficult habit to break. Even a shooter with proper trigger control will often start flinching eventually, after firing enough rounds to become either fatigued or oversensitive to the recoil pulse. If this happens to you, take a break or end the session.

Low shots indicate a flinch. This can show up late in the practice session from shooter fatigue.

The best method I have seen for eliminating the flinch is to not allow the subconscious mind to know exactly when the piece will discharge. This method is called the "surprise break." Simply put, you'll pull the trigger gradually enough so that the exact instant of firing comes as a surprise to you. Your subconscious cannot direct a flinch action, then, because we don't know just when the gun will fire.

To effect the surprise break, we must first start with a fairly slow trigger pull, one that takes place over a period of several seconds. With time and practice, this interval will be shortened more and more until you have a fairly quick trigger motion, even though your mind will have been trained to still sense

You should have no more tension in your gun grip than you would in a slightly firm handshake with a woman. A bone-crushing John Wayne grip is a no-no.

the time interval involved and still not know the exact instant of discharge. This requires constant practice to achieve, but, eventually, you can fire shots in fractions of a second. The mind will have been trained to consider that even such a short time interval carries in it the uncertainty of when the shot will fire, and the flinch action will be kept at bay.

How do you know if you're not flinching? If you see your muzzle flash or see your front sight lifting in recoil, you can be pretty sure you are not flinching. Either visual will allow you to call your shot in your own mind, and without viewing the actual hits on the target.

The counterpoint to all this is the yanking, mashing, and jerking of the trigger. Not only does this impart a violent physical impulse to the gun, it is also a prime enabler of the flinch. A desire to force speed causes this problem. That desire, or impatience, comes from an inability to hold the sight alignment on the desired target aim point. The gun weaves all around and, when the sights cross the aiming point, there may be an overwhelming desire to yank the trigger at just that instant. Don't do it! Instead, consider this alternate method. Every time the sights cross your desired aiming point, add a little pressure to the trigger, maybe a half-pound at most, and not enough to fire the gun. When the sights weave off your aiming point, stop adding pressure, but continue to hold the pressure you already have, rather than releasing it. When the gun weaves back to your aim point, add a few more ounces. Maintain this schedule, and, at some point, the gun will fire as you add the last few needed ounces while the sights are lined up. It will be a surprise, and it will happen only when the sights are on the desired point of aim.

A father pressing the trigger for his daughter to eliminate shooter flinch. He is also able to check for her accuracy of aiming this way.

One other aspect of trigger control deals with the motion of the finger after the shot is fired. Ideally, you should let the trigger finger forward only enough to allow the trigger mechanism to reset itself. The finger should stay in contact with the surface of the trigger, not move forwards off of it. In this manner, the motion of the trigger finger is minimized. Also, try not to fling your finger all the way forwards, off the trigger and to the front of the trigger guard. This is pointless, unnecessary, and wastes both time and motion.

The best results are obtained when all the above tactics are combined. The proper grip on the pistol, proper placement of the finger pad on the trigger, the relaxation of the trigger hand, the independent and proper motion of the trigger finger, the relaxation of the mind, and the surprise break all work together to produce a firing action that will not disturb your perfect sight picture at the moment of discharge.

From a safety standpoint, the trigger finger should be clear of the trigger and held straight outside the trigger guard at all times until the sights are aligned on the target (Rule 3). When we retract or lower the gun from the aiming position to the ready position, we move our trigger finger off the trigger. If we're shooting a pistol with a manual safety, like the 1911, we also thumb the safety to the "on" position at this time. If another shot is to be taken, keep both hands on the gun in the proper grip and bring it back to the mid-chest position with the barrel pointed downrange and slightly toward the ground. When extending the gun for the next shot, that is the time that the safety is disengaged, hammer cocked, etc., as the gun first starts moving upwards and outwards, so you are ready to shoot by the time the gun is brought into your line of sight. (Proper movement of the gun from either the holster or the ready position to the aiming position and back will be fully covered in following chapters.)

With a hammer-cocking trigger pull, such as that on a double-action revolver or semi-auto, we need to be able to exert considerable force through nearly an inch of motion. This unavoidably imparts motion to the gun, making this technique largely unsuitable for a very precise shot and much more difficult to master. There are ways, however.

First, we need to train and strengthen the trigger finger to perform this long hard pull with minimum disturbance to the gun. A high volume of dry-fire practice can accomplish this.

Second, there are two ways to deal with the pull. You can have either a long, steady, continuous pull until the hammer drops, or it can be a "staged" pull. The staged pull brings the finger about three-quarters of the way back, or to the point just before the hammer is released. There the finger pauses for an instant, while the shooter steadies the gun and verifies the sight picture. At this point, the small remaining part of the pull is applied, which has minimal effect on the sight picture. With a great deal of practice, staging can be done at a speed almost as fast as that with a straight-through pull.

> *Trigger mastery requires a great deal of practice. Fortunately, much can be accomplished (at no cost!) with an unloaded gun and dry-fire practice.*

Trigger mastery requires a great deal of attentiveness to the details just presented, and a great deal of practice. Fortunately, much of this practice can be done simply through dry-fire practice, which is "firing" an empty, unloaded gun. In this kind of practice, you go through all the mechanics of firing a shot, but, of course, you'll hear only a click instead of a bang. (Make absolutely sure your gun is unloaded, including chambers and magazines, perform your practice in the safest possible direction within your domicile, and don't keep live ammo in the same room in which you're practicing.) There are lots of benefits to dry-fire practice; there's no noise, no recoil, no distractions, no emotional baggage, no motivation to flinch. A high volume of dry-fire, especially by a beginner, will make an enormous difference in skill acquisition.

Eventually, you will reach the point of having a totally subconscious trigger pull reflex, in which seeing the correct sight picture for the shot will cause your trigger finger to fire the gun without any conscious thought process, an act that will occur literally faster than you can consciously think about it. This is what enables shot-to-shot split times—the time span in between shots—to get down to around $2/10$-second, sometimes even faster, among accomplished competitive shooters.

BREATHING

Ideally, you should hold your breath when firing. The motion of breathing imparts motion to the gun. There is some evidence that holding your breath after exhaling results in greater steadiness, and doing so also follows the natural cycle of your unconscious breathing, so it is something you can do without much thought or disruption of your natural breathing habit. This is how shooting accurately with a rifle is accomplished. At first this will be difficult, especially if you are taking extra time to aim and develop a slow trigger pull to maintain the surprise break. You should also be aware that holding your breath for more than about eight seconds will start to degrade your eyesight and physical performance. If you run out of air on a shot, don't rush the shot. Instead, lower the gun, breathe regularly again, and start over. If you must breath with the gun extended in the firing position, do so from your lower abdomen, not your upper chest, as this will impart less motion to the gun.

Eventually, your speed will be great enough that the handgun can be raised, aimed, and fired within a second or so. At that point, simply pausing your breathing motion for that second is easily accomplished.

CHAPTER 4

THE MODERN ISOSCELES STANCE AND TECHNIQUE

"The basis for the Modern Isosceles lies in how the gun is gripped, aided and abetted by the posture of your entire body. Perfected, it allows for incredible shooting speeds."

The modern technique of two-handed pistol shooting for speed, recoil control, and accuracy uses a grip and stance that enable the quickest and most effortless recoil recovery.

The development, by Jack Weaver, of the Weaver stance, in the 1950s, and its adoption by Col. Jeff Cooper as part of his Modern Technique of the Pistol, were great leaps forward in pistol shooting. Then, in the late 1980s, competitor Rob Leatham developed another technique called the "Modern Isosceles," whose slightly improved efficiency allowed its creator to dominate practical shooting competition for years (Leatham is still the man to beat, and recently won his fifth World IPSC Championship).

Leatham's grip and stance allow for shooting at incredible speeds, even with a powerful gun like the .45 semi-automatic pistol. This technique has been adopted by almost all competitive shooters and is slowly working its way into the police and military world. Its effectiveness comes from its management of recoil energy and is the most efficient method yet developed.

The basis of this technique lies in how the gun is gripped, aided and abetted by the posture of the entire body. With apologies to Mr. Leatham, as I did not learn this directly from him and I had to do my own analysis of how and why it works, what follows may not be "gospel." However, it still works brilliantly, so let's proceed. We'll start with the hands.

THE GRIP

The proper grip of the firing hand is described in the prior chapter on trigger management. It should be kept in mind that, as important as the trigger-finger hand grip is, the grip of the supporting hand is also quite particular. First, it requires that the support hand be tilted downwards to about the fullest extent of wrist flexibility. When this hand is gripping the gun, its thumb should be horizontal or parallel to the gun barrel. If the forefinger were to be extended, it should point as nearly straight forward as possible. The heel of the support hand palm should be placed against the stock panel on the left side (for right-handed shooters) of the pistol—*not* on top of the heel of the trigger hand—and the prominent bone at the very base of the support thumb (at the wrist) should tuck under the last joint of the firing hand thumb.

The support thumb should not bear on the pistol, but, instead, should point straight ahead and be relaxed. The grip pressure of the support-hand thumb does not come from the digit itself, but rather from the meaty pad at its base. The pairing of thumbs—trigger-hand thumb above, support-hand thumb lower—should provide complete contact between the two, without any gaps between them. Note the picture showing the proper grip with alignment lines drawn on the

shooter's thumbs (this neat trick comes from Matt Burkett's *Practical Shooting* training videos). If your support hand starts to slip from the downwards-tilted position to a more normal position, a gap will be created between your thumbs, and your support-hand thumb will tend to point upwards at about a 45-degree angle. Watch for this and correct it when you see it. Draw lines on your thumbs to monitor your grip. Remember that the knuckle at the base of the support-hand thumb is not part of the alignment, rather it's the end joint of the trigger-hand thumb and the wrist area of the support-hand thumb that are used. The grip force of the trigger hand should be concentrated on the front and back of the gun, while the grip force of the support hand should be applied from side to side. In this manner, the gun butt has grip force applied to it on all four sides.

If the gun is a 1911-type semi-auto, the trigger-hand thumb should stay on top of the safety, while the support hand should ride high enough to create the seamless thumb-to-thumb contact I just talked about. Keep your support-hand forefinger off the front of the trigger guard, as such a hand configuration and placement do nothing to help and actually weaken the overall grip. Keep in mind, too, that, with a 1911, this high grip often makes the palm of the trigger hand somewhat retract from

Lines designate where your thumb knuckles should align.

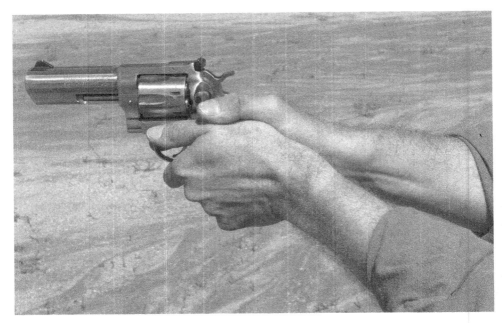

A proper revolver grip.

The Modern Isosceles ready stance (left photo), and in full extension viewed from the right. Note the forward lean, foot spacing, shoulders pushed towards target, pistol at eye level, and unlocked elbows.

the grip safety at the back of the frame, and if the hand is retracted so that the safety is precluded from being depressed enough, the gun will not fire.

Remember to get your hand not only high up, but also as far *into* the backstrap of the gun as it will go. If this is difficult for you, know that many grip safeties can be modified by a build-up of material on the saftey's lower end, or the entire unit can be replaced with one that is already manufactured with extra thickness there. Such modifications can be worthwhile, as a high grip allows substantially greater control over the gun than does a low thumb grip.

The pressure applied by each hand is critical. As I've already discussed, the shooting hand should be fairly relaxed. The support hand should provide a very strong grip. A simple rule that works well is to grip with the support hand tight enough to induce tremors, then relax it just enough so that the tremors go away. What you have left is the grip pressure you want.

The purpose of this grip is to induce a static tension in the hands, wrists, and forearms. It is this tension of both grip and

The Modern Isosceles stance from the front (left photo) and as viewed from the shooter's left side. Note shoulder-width foot spacing and overlapping fingers.

canted support hand that brings the gun back from recoil automatically, without the shooter having to do anything deliberately. In short, your hands act like rubber bands that snap the gun back down from recoil just as fast as it bounced upwards. This is not a pushing action by the shooter; the shooter merely maintains proper grip tension throughout the firing cycle.

This grip tension in each hand has an important affect upon the recoil recovery of the gun. If too little strength is used, the gun will kick up sharply and not return to your desired sight picture, due to the lack of elastic tension. If too much strength is used, the gun will kick up less, but still not return, because of too much stiffness in the hands and wrists. If this is problematic, experiment with differing amounts of tension in your

A shooter in training with a Ruger GP100 revolver in .357 Magnum.

s, always remembering that the trigger hand should provide the
er grip of the two. When you see your gun recover instantly
the recoil back to the sight picture you had before the shot, you
it right.

s an aside, avoid loosening and re-
ing your support hand fingers after each
some people do this unconsciously, for
reason. Keep the support hand tight and
)ving throughout the string of shots.

STANCE

1e elbows of the extended arms should
ghtly bent, not locked; some flexing
uired at these joints. Locked elbows
mit an uncomfortable recoil jolt back to
10ulders, and can be painful to the elbow

> *The grip tension in each hand has an important affect upon the recoil recovery of the gun. When you see your gun recover instantly back to the sight picture you had before the shot, you have it right.*

. The arms should be rotated so that the points of the elbows
irected mostly downwards, rather than out to the sides. This
oning allows the arms to act like pistons, transferring recoil
upper torso, while the unlocked elbows help absorb some of
coil energy into the arms themselves. The shoulders should be
d slightly towards the target. This has the affect of rounding
)per back a bit. Bend forwards slightly from the waist while
this.
1e desired result is that the upper body is slightly curved, with
10ulders ahead of the hips; your nose should be over your toes.
in turn, places more of your body mass in a position in line with
coil. It is a slight amount, but make sure your upper body weight
biased forwards. This is one of the factors that helps in absorb-
1d controlling recoil. If you are fully erect, recoil will eventu-
ush you backwards and off balance, as well as force your arms
rds and out of line with the target. If your weight stays forward,
other hand, your body will tend to return to this position after
bing the recoil pulse.
e right amount of forward lean for each shooter will be found
gh experimentation. How the gun recoils in your hands, how
)vers, and how much it pushes you back will determine your
rd lean. Use the amount of lean that best tames the gun and
nizes your upper body positioning displacement. The idea is
1trol the pistol's recoil movement, rather than the pistol's recoil
)lling your movement. Be the boss of the gun, not vice versa.
ace your feet about shoulder width apart and place your feet so
1e foot on the trigger-hand side is rearwards of the support-side
)ut only so that the toe of the rear foot is no further forwards
he heel of the leading foot. Do not allow your feet to come too
together, as this will negatively affect your balance. Also, hav-

Below: Getting the grip correct. The trigger hand should be as high on the frame as possible.

Right: And again. Check those lines on the thumbs.

ing your feet spaced correctly will allow you to move in any direction, very quickly, if necessary. This balance and movement ability might save your life in a self-defense situation. Bend your knees and lower your body some to allow your rear end to stick out slightly. This, in turn, allows your shoulders to round towards the target more easily and helps keep your upper body weight biased forwards. Lean your whole body forward a few inches from your ankle joints, so that not only your upper body, but also your hips and thighs move forward. Remember that you are absorbing force coming at you from the front, so lean into it! However, do not go into an exaggerated crouch, and make sure to keep your face over your lead

A range officer runs a shooter through a practical shooting match under the auspices of the U.S. Practical Shooting Association (USPSA), also called "IPSC" (pronounced "ipsick") shooting, for the International Practical Shooting Confederation. A good forward-leaning stance helps counter recoil.

foot toes. Remember, too, to relax the rest of your body from the elbows back to your feet. Excess tension in the shoulders, arms, abdomen, or back will interfere with the proper management of recoil.

PRESENTATION OF THE GUN FROM READY TO AIMING

There are two basic parts to the Modern Isosceles stance. First is the ready position, where the gun is retracted back to the chest. Second is the actual aiming part, whereby the gun is in front of the body with the arms fully extended.

Another shooter runs the practical course. Note the forward rounding of his back and shoulders.

In the ready position, the safety is in the on position, with the thumb on top of it for a 1911-style gun, trigger finger straight along the outside of the trigger guard; for a double-action semi-auto or revolver, the hammer is in the upright or forward position.

The act of extending the gun to the aiming position is called the "presentation." Kelly McCann, in his excellent *Crucible* series of training tapes, has come up with a nifty technique to let you start aiming as soon as possible. As you present the gun, you should first bring it upwards quickly to the sight line between the eye and target, so that you can see your sights as quickly as possible—but this should be done before your arms move forward any further than to get the gun in front of your face. In this manner, you will see your sights

> *The right amount of forward lean for each shooter will be found through experimentation. Use the amount of lean that best tames the gun and minimizes upper body displacement.*

(Opposite and this page) In recoil. Note the empty case above shooter's forehead. In this case, the shooter's wrists remain straight, while the forearms flex upward at the elbows. What you want is the opposite, to reduce gun deflection off the target and speed recovery. Proper grip tension is key.

This stance is too upright.

A little forward lean, but too erect overall.

An awkward stance.

This stance is just about right.

well before your arms reach full extension, and it is at this point that you will transfer your eye focus from the target to the front sight and place your finger on the trigger.

Now, move the gun smoothly forward to full arm extension, while looking at your sights and checking alignment. Since the gun will be in motion, your sight picture will not be perfect, but, with this technique, you can make a coarse correction and have the alignment of front and rear sights and their alignment with the target, very close to what you need while the gun is still moving forward. By the time you reach full extension, the gun will already be in your sight line, your focus will already be on the front sight, the sights will

The ready position, shown from the side.

already be superimposed on the place you want the bullet to go, and you will already have checked your sight picture. If you do everything right, you not only can fire an accurate shot the instant the gun stops extending, you may be able to fire a good shot even while the gun is still moving forward. This is much faster than extending the gun at an angle out from the chest, whereby the gun's sights don't enter your sight line until full extension has been achieved.

THE PRESENTATION-CREATED SIGHT PICTURE

There is one thing you must understand about the presentation, and that is that you don't just bring the gun to where your eye is looking, then start aiming. You must train your hands to bring the gun to where your eyes are looking *with correct sight alignment and sight picture,* instantly. You verify the sight picture with the instant "flash sight picture." In other words, when your eyes pick out the spot where you want the bullet to hit, the pistol must suddenly appear there, ready to fire a perfectly accurate shot. *The accurate correct sight picture is already created by the hands at presentation; it is not a function of fiddling around and seeking with the sights.* This is of extreme importance, and it does not come without a lot of practice.

There are other things you will do during presentation. One of these is to push off the safety on a 1911-type gun as soon as the gun starts moving from the ready position. When you do this, you'll leave your thumb on top of the safety lever. The trigger finger can start to move to the trigger as the gun comes into your line of sight. If, on the other hand, you have a double-action trigger-cocking gun and are starting the presentation with the hammer down, you can start a controlled partial press on the trigger to begin moving the hammer rearwards as the sights come into view. *This must not be overdone*, since we do not want a premature discharge. What we want is to bring the hammer about half-way back as the sights come into view. Full pressure can then be applied, when you see the correct sight picture.

When practicing, first get your grip correctly on the gun while you're in the ready position, then check your stance, starting at your feet and working up to your hands, where you'll re-check your thumb lines. By this time, everything should be correct and you can finish presenting the gun to the aiming position and focus on aiming and firing without worrying about anything else.

There is a *natural* point of aim with this pistol stance.

Raise the gun to eye level, without extending it fully forward. Shift your focus to the front sight and then push the gun forward.

Try first working in this stance without a precise aiming point—just let the pistol point where it wants to, straight ahead at nothing in particular. See where it wants to go generally. Once you know where the gun tends to point for you, work with an aiming point. Lock your eyes onto the aiming point, then present the pistol, bringing your pistol sights into your sight line. Next, try locking your eyes onto the aiming point, then close your eyes, present the pistol, and open up your eyes again. See how far off your body put the pistol from the target. Readjust your stance orientation with your feet for right or left and try again. This will help you to "address the target" with your body stance

The gun at eye level, with the shooter extending their arms. This provides time to evaluate the sight picture.

as you spot the target and face it. Eventually, you will be able to bring the pistol to bear at whatever your eyes are looking at, instantly and reflexively.

The end result of using the Modern Isosceles is that the gun muzzle will jump up place, and the muzzle will snap right back down to your normal aiming position, *with correct sight alignment and sight picture,* without you having to do a thing. This is what allows fast shooting. Practice the above consistently, slowly, and patiently, until you can see your front sight sharply, fire without flinching or otherwise disturbing the gun, and so you see your front sight track up and down in recoil so that it quickly returns to its starting point after the shot. *Seeing the gun move up and down in recoil, seeing the front sight snap back down to a motionless position and the sight alignment created after recoil, is critical to the process.* This is what places you in control

The author demonstrates the proper stance at an IPSC shoot with his 9mm. Not only is he handsome, witty, and urbane, he's also a darn good shot.

of follow-up shots at high speed—you can see and verify through the flash sight picture that the pistol recovers from recoil right back to a proper sight picture. This is what allows development of high-speed subconscious sight picture verification and subconscious trigger press.

This shooter is leaning too far back in his stance. He's also using the old cup-and-saucer hold. Neither his body position nor his grip offer any recoil dampening benefits.

A stance too upright can permit too much muzzle rise. Note that the arms are forced up from the shoulder joints, which brings the pistol far off target. The arms should not rise in recoil, but rather move rearwards, like pistons.

A front view of the classic Weaver grip, which uses a push/pull isometric grip to control recoil.

CHAPTER 5

PERFECTING THE FUNDAMENTALS

"Every shot you take, fast or slow, near or far, small or large target, requires the correct fundamentals."

The fundamentals are everything. Without them you cannot hit your target. Forget about speed, because that will come with training. A fast miss on a large, close target solves nothing. Ditto, a slow miss on a small distant target. *Every* shot you take, fast or slow, near or far, small or large target, requires the correct fundamentals.

What are the fundamentals? Here's a summation:

- Correct grip—remember those lines drawn on the thumbs in the previous chapter—and relative grip pressures.
- Correct stance with forward weight bias, when shooting from the standing position.
- Correct gun presentation that locks your sights onto whatever your eys are looking at.
- Correct use of front sight focus and the flash sight picture for verification of correct presentation.
- Correct trigger press, without flinching or jerking.
- Correct follow-through of calling the shot, seeing the full recoil cycle with sight picture realized again, and minimum trigger reset motion.

Read all that over 10 times. Then read it over another thousand. Make sure it sinks in.

You will be quizzed by reality. If you are lucky, it will be in the form of your practice target results. If you are very unlucky, your quiz will be in the form of an armed enemy intent on harming you—if this last one happens, your failing grade will not arrive in a red "F" marked on a piece of paper.

DRY-FIRE FIRST DRILLS

Your basic drill at this point will be to set your grip correctly on the gun, bring it to the ready position (pointing downrange and below eye level, just in front of your chest), set your stance from feet to hands, present the gun as we've already describe, making sure you transition your eye focus to the front sight at the earliest possible time before reaching full arm extension. Make sure your finger is off the trigger until your eyes find the sights. Your goal is to first achieve correct sight alignment *with your hands*, focusing on the front sight to verify as perfect alignment as possible between front and rear sights. Once you have that, press the trigger without disturbing your aim.

Why do I keep repeating this? Because you need to repeat it to perfect your presentation and hits. It is of critical importance that you understand that, at this stage in your learning, you are teaching your hands to present and instantly align the gun correctly with your line of sight and your intended target. Perfecting this produces the flash sight picture you'll need to make fast, accurate hits. Yes, this will take lots and lots of practice. Get cracking.

> *Your goal is to first achieve correct sight alingnment with your hands. Why do I keep repeating this? Because you need to repeat it to perfect it.*

Start performing your drill with one of the best practice techniques available to you, dry-fire. It costs nothing at all but time. With dry-fire practice, you'll start by picking the safest inside your home (or on a range) at which you may aim your gun. A block wall of your basement or garage is the ideal setup. Why all the concern about a safe backstop for dry-fire, when there's not going to be any actual firing? Because every once in a great while, someone will make a mistake!

The concept of dry-fire practicing is that you'll go through all the motions of firing a shot with a completely empty gun. You must make sure that the chamber and magazines of an autoloader, and all the chambers on a revolver, are void of ammunition, and best practices insist you should keep any live ammo in a different room altogether.

How do you know your dry-fire practice is producing the desired results? When the hammer falls with a click and your sights do not move, you're doing it right. How often should you dry-fire practice? Master Class shooters dry-fire practice all the time, some every day, but for you, working on establishing and perfecting the fundamentals, work dry-fire practice into your schedule two or three times a week for at least 20 minutes at a time. I would even recommend you do this before you even try going to the range for the first time, and, when you do go to the range, dry-fire for a few minutes before you load up with live ammo. It's a good way to get warmed up and start your live-fire shooting with the right habits going forward.

LIVE-FIRE FIRST DRILLS

In your initial live-fire session, start by shooting one shot. Watch your gun's sights cycle in recoil, confirm the post-recoil sight picture, then bring the gun back to the ready position, applying the safety, if applicable. Repeat until you have burned up your ammo for the first session, at least 50 to 100 rounds. Yes, going over your basics just one shot at a time can be boring, but be patient! You are building the foundation of the most basic and necessary pistol skills there are.

Once you feel you've successfully identified your sight picture after recoil, move on to the next live-fire drill. In this one, you'll fire two shots at your aim point for each single gun presentation. As you did with the single-shot drill, watch the gun cycle fully and recreate the sight picture, then press off the second shot, following through once again to verify the post-recoil sight picture. Then bring the gun back to ready.

One of the things to work on through both these drills is to get the surprise break on the trigger and not blink during the shot. This will allow you to call your shot, see your sight lift in recoil, and see how your sight picture reassembles itself automatically. This last bit is controlled by the relative grip power in your hands, so that is what you will use as a gauge; if the gun does not return to the proper sight picture after recoil, adjust your grip until it does.

Working with a target that has a small, precise aiming point, say, a one- or two-inch circle, begin your initial live-fire drills from a distance of just three yards. Do not fret if you cannot hold the gun perfectly steady on your aim point—almost no one can! So relax. Remember to avoid snatching at the trigger when the sights cross the center of your aiming point. If you are too wobbly even at three yards, use the technique described in the previous chapter for adding and holding pressure as you move through the aiming point. And again, make each shot a surprise through slow, gentle trigger finger pressure.

Watch your gun's sight cycle in recoil, confirm the post-recoil sight picture, then bring the gun back to the ready position. Repeat. Repeat. Repeat.

If you perform the first one- and two-shot drills correctly, your shots should group very closely at three yards after only

a few rounds of practice. When your shots all go into a small ragged hole, move the target back to five yards, then seven, 10, and, eventually, 15 yards. At the further distances, you'll likely need a bigger aiming point and you won't be getting small ragged holes anymore, but, if your groups are fist-sized or smaller at seven yards and can easily be covered by both hands at 15, you are on the right track, as far as execution of the fundamentals goes.

You cannot worry about the "cooler" aspects of shooting—speed, multiple targets, movement, etc.—at this point. All those things will come in time. At this point, you must create the foundational skill set that will be applied to those more advance skills. If you don't do that now, you'll just be wasting ammo later. Patience!

The low shots indicate the onset of a flinch. If this is happeng to you after you've been shooting a while, stop your session, give yourself a rest before going back, or pack up your gear and hit the range again tomorrow.

GETTING THE BASICS DOWN: SELF-DIAGNOSIS

Pay close attention to what you see in the sight picture and what you feel in your grip, trigger finger motion, and stance. What you feel and see here can help you diagnose errors in your form and move you on to perfection. Truth is, you will occasionally throw a wild shot. We all do. But don't let this discourage you. Rather, use each bad shot as a learning experience.

Let's say you mismanaged the trigger pull in some way. Use the location of the shots to diagnose what you did wrong. If you were flinching, your shots will go low. You will also probably be blinking at the same time, so you won't have seen your front sight lift in recoil.

In another kind of miss, you may be squeezing your whole hand, which drives the shot usually left for a right-hander (right for a left-hander), and sometimes down, as well. Or you may be pushing or pulling the gun to either side with trigger finger motion. Dry-fire a bit to see if your sights are moved by the motion of the trigger finger.

If your sight picture wasn't correct, the shot could go anywhere. Learn to make sure you're seeing your sights clearly at the instant of discharge. If you are seeing them clearly, you will know of any misalignment and will see where the shot will go even before you look at the target—you will have "called the shot." If you can't call your shot, your eye focus might not be sharp enough on the sights (perhaps it was somewhere between the front sight and the target), or you might not have even been looking at your sights at all, because you were focused on the target.

A wide shot, possibly from a whole-hand clench while pulling the trigger, a powerful flinch, or losing focus on the front sight.

Your grip pressure or hand position could be incorrect. This will make the gun return from recoil in the wrong position. If the gun recoils up and to one side, it may be due to the hand on that side having excessive grip pressure. Follow through the shot and watch the gun track up and down in recoil while you experiment with different hand pressures. Remember that the shooting hand must have the weaker grip, the support hand must be sharply canted down, and the gun should track straight up and down.

If you are consistently shooting high, you may be flinching, which will push on the rear bottom of the gun butt and drive the muzzle upwards slightly. If you're not flinching, you may be looking at the front sight over the top of the rear sight, rather than through the rear sight notch, or you may simply looking over the top of both sights.

There are many ways to make mistakes. The good thing is that it is quite simple and easy to make corrections. Always strive to be patient and relaxed both mentally and physically,

What you want to see at seven to 10 yards, though this group should be placed a couple inches higher.

Good shots in the tight upper A-zone.

even if you are having a rough session. Go back over the above descriptions of technique regularly to make sure you are doing everything from stance to grip to aiming to trigger pull correctly.

> *You must see your sights clearly at the moment the shot is discharged. Only when you've perfected this can you call your shots.*

KNOWING WHEN TO STOP

Shooting requires considerable mental concentration, as well as physical stamina. No matter your practice regimen—once a day, once a week, once a month—at some point you will start getting tired. This will appear on the target as an increasing number of bad shots, usually of the flinch variety, and, if you keep on going, you will simply be ingraining bad habits. So, when you see your shots consistently start to go astray, take a break of at least 10 to 15 minutes and relax for a while. If that doesn't help, go home. Really. One of the worst things you can do is keep training as you're falling apart. You will only gain the negative. When you can't do it correctly anymore, stop!

Following the regimen of practice I've described, a basic level of competence may be achieved in as few as two or three range sessions for some people, though it can take a lot more for others. Also realize that, for a beginner, these skills will vanish if you put the gun away. It takes *thousands* of rounds of dry- and live-fire over a long period to really ingrain skills that stick through periods of your gun potentially collecting dust in the future. So, until you become truly competent, dry-fire and shoot on a regular schedule as often as you can. The gun by itself has small value. It is your skill with it that makes it a beneficial tool.

CHAPTER 6

THE DRAW

"What we really want is not speed of the gun from the holster to the extended position, but rather speed from the holster to our line of sight."

Assuming we carry a handgun for self-defense, we might find ourselves in a situation that requires its usage in a hurry. Failure to perform quickly in such situations can cost us our lives. With this in mind, the gun carrier needs to develop a smooth and efficient draw stroke, one that incorporates a good and proper strong-hand grip on the gun at first touch, a smooth motion to clear the holster, and an efficient movement of the gun into our line of sight so that a sight picture can be acquired as quickly as possible.

There are various approaches to drawing, including short motions that bring the gun barely out of the holster for use in engaging targets at arm's length or less. There are also many different ways to position a holster. For simplicity's sake, I will concentrate on the basic draw motion from a strong-side belt holster, a draw that brings the gun to eye level for sight acquisition, using the two-hand hold as previously described. This gives us the greatest odds for firing accurately in a short time period. Remember, a fast miss solves nothing and merely gives our opponent a better chance to shoot us first.

The shortest distance between two points is a straight line, so one would think that motion of the gun in a straight line from the holster to the extended position might be the best. However, such a movement doesn't allow us to see our sights until the gun has reached that extended point. What we really want is not speed of the gun from the holster to the extended position, but rather speed from the holster to our line of sight.

To do this, we want to bring the gun from the holster upwards in a fairly steep line, so as to place the gun in our sight

This is where you start, when practicing drawing from a holster. Relax! Keep your arms, hands, and fingers loose. Your feet are shoulder width apart, your upper body upright. Everything is balanced.

Strong hand gripping the gun, weak hand in the grab position, shown from the front. Note the hands move together to grip and grab.

Strong hand gripping the gun, weak hand in grab position, shown from right.

Clear the holster. Note the straight trigger finger at this stage of the presentation.

Rotate the muzzle downrange and bring the gun toward the support hand, form your complete grip, and disengage the safety (if necessary).

Raise your gun up to eyesight line, close in to the face and with a high trigger-side elbow. Shift your focus to the front sight and form your flash sight picture.

Extend your arms fully, maintaining your focus on the flash sight picture.

line and fairly close to our face in as little time as possible. This is the "straight line" we are concerned with, not the one from the gun's muzzle to the target. Once the gun's sights are in your sight line, you'll transfer your focus to the sights and then drive the gun forwards along that sight line and out to the fully extended position; you will remain focused on your sights throughout the extension. This allows for the correction of any errors in the sight picture at the earliest possible time and also permits us to reach the extended position ready to fire the shot (or even before that, if necessary), having already formed the correct flash sight picture.

Refining the draw in this manner enables firing at a very close target before the gun is fully extended, but while still having a sight picture. This technique is taught by Kelly McCann in his *Crucible* video training series. He recommends keeping the strong-side elbow high (upper arm staying as horizontal to the ground as possible), as the gun is brought to the line of sight and as it starts moving forwards. Letting your strong-side elbow droop during the draw stroke causes your arm and the gun to droop out of your sight line.

OUT OF THE HOLSTER

One of the first actions in the draw is to move both hands simultaneously. The gun (trigger-pulling) hand must grip the gun in the same manner you will use to shoot it as soon as you grasp the gun in the holster. There will be no time to change your grip during the draw and presentation, so it is absolutely necessary to achieve a proper firing grip at first touch. This takes quite a bit of practice, but its importance cannot be overlooked. *Get your hand on the gun butt in the correct firing grip.*

It is probably best to have your hand approach the gun butt from above, rather than from the side, to effect the centering of the butt in the web of your hand. Make sure that your trigger finger is straight along the outside of the holster over the trigger guard! The firing hand thumb, after popping any thumbsnap strap your holster may have, should be "flagged" or sticking up in the hitchhiker position. This keeps it from accidentally nudging off the safety on a cocked and locked 1911-style pistol while the gun's still in the holster and also keeps it from getting fouled on any straps or snaps in the way. If your holster has a thumbsnap strap, your hand should come straight down onto the top of the gun butt with the thumb

> You must grip the gun in the same manner you will you use to shoot it, as soon as you grab it in the holster. There will not be time to change your grip during the draw and presentation.

flagged but pointing forwards slightly. In this manner, it will pop the snap as you achieve your grip.

If your holster has an outside snap strap, rather than one topside, you will have to release it with the outside or leading edge of the base of the trigger finger while sweeping your hand upwards along the outside of the holster. Then the hand rises slightly above the gun butt and drops straight down onto it.

The position of your holster may require certain other specific positioning of your drawing hand. If the holster is a strong-side, high-ride, behind-the-hip concealment belt holster, the gun will be positioned high and around toward your back somewhat. You may have to raise up your gun-side shoulder and rotate your hand towards the gun butt to get a proper firing grip, such that your palm is more facing your kidney (where the gun butt is). To effect a proper grip in this case, you'll have to have your flagged thumb point out to the side, rather than forwards.

Remember, you must achieve the proper firing grip on the gun butt *the first time*. Apply this grip while the gun is in the holster and then analyze just how your arm, hand, and shoulder have to be positioned to apply it correctly. This is what you will practice to achieve, every time you draw. If you mess it up, it will ruin the entire process all the way through the shot, as an incorrect grip will both cause misalignment of the gun in the firing position and defeat the eventual, repetition-ingrained, correct muscle memory that produces the instantaneous and automatic alignment of the gun in a high-speed presentation.

What's your non-shooting hand doing at this time? The support hand moves at the same time as the gun hand. As the latter reaches for the gun, the former moves across the body to a position just under the strong-side pectoral muscle. The inside of your support forearm should be horizontal across your chest. The wrist should be bent with the palm facing sideways to the strong side, and the hand canted downward with the thumb extended straight ahead and the fingers pointing as nearly straight downwards to the ground as possible. When the draw motion starts, it should look like there is a string tied between both wrists—the hands move together. The support hand ends up in a place that is along the path of the gun as it comes up from and out of the holster and towards the line of sight. This position is called the "grab."

As your hands are moving into the grip (gun hand) and grab (support hand) positions, you should assume your shooting posture as related in the chapter on the Modern Isosceles stance. Bend your knees slightly, stick your fanny out slightly, and lean your upper body slightly towards the target. If your feet started out in an awkward position, move them so they are about shoulder-width apart and with the trigger hand-sided foot to the

A proper stance established, this young shooter clears the holster, and you can see her support hand coming in for the grab.

rear. All these movements should be done simultaneously with your hand motions. By the time your hands are in the grip and grab positions, your body should be in the position from which you will shoot. No further body movement (besides the arms) should need to take place after this point. In other words, don't bob and weave back and forth as you bring the gun out of the holster to the shooting position.

Draw the gun out of the holster in line with the angle at which the holster holds the gun. Any other angle or any twisting or other motion will cause the gun to bind in the holster. Keep in mind that, with a high-ride holster, you will probably need to raise your strong-side shoulder up pretty high as well, to help your arm move enough get the gun all the way out of the holster. Try to keep your gun-arm elbow pointing rearwards, as opposed to letting it swing out to the side. This helps align your hand with the gun butt and also prevents wasted motion. Also, as mentioned before, keep the strong-side elbow high as the gun comes up to our line of sight, to avoid a lowered elbow pulling the rest of the arm (and gun) downwards with it.

As the gun comes up towards your support hand, the gun should be rotated muzzle-downrange just before it intercepts the

Once the grip is established (left), the shooter rotates the muzzle downrange.

support hand. For a 1911-style gun, your thumb should be on top of the safety (but not disengaging it) as the pistol clears the holster. As the muzzle gets pointed downrange, now you can disengage the manual safety if your gun has one. For a 1911-style, your thumb should stay up on top of the manual safety lever as part of your normal firing grip.

Make sure the support hand does not present itself in front of the path of the muzzle as you draw the gun and orient it downrange. To do so is called "sweeping." Use the gun and strong hand to sort of scoop up the support hand from its position in front of your chest.

Another thing not to do? Do not reach out with both hands separately and "clap" them out in front of you. This takes too long and causes the gun to wobble when your hands come together. Bring the gun through the support hand position, get your correct support hand grip as described in the Modern Isosceles section, and continue raising the gun up towards your jawline.

At this point, with a proper two-handed grip but before you begin extending your arms, your trigger finger should still be off the trigger and straight along the side of the gun. This is

Raising up the gun and beginning to extend it forward.

Finally, the gun fully extended and at eye level. Find your flash sight picture and press the trigger.

almost identical to the ready position described previously, except the gun starts from the strong side of the body and has to move across your body to your center-line. At this time you should also be looking at the exact spot on your target you want the bullet to hit. Now, drive the gun upwards and slightly forwards fully into your line of sight, so that your sights become superimposed on your target. Do not make an upwards or downwards arc with the gun throughout this process; you are not bowling or casting a fishing line.

Focus on your sights before your arms are fully extended! This is your head start on aiming, and it can help you engage close targets accurately.

The idea is to move the gun quickly straight up into your line of sight and then smoothly straight forwards towards the target.

If you have a double-action (trigger-cocking) semi-auto or revolver, you may start trigger pressure to bring the hammer partway back once you see your sights. Teach yourself a slow, partial trigger pull here so as not to fire the pistol prematurely.

Now for the crucial ingredient. As the gun sights come into your line of sight, transfer your focus to the front sight and let the target blur slightly. This is of the utmost importance. The faster you see your sights, the faster you can verify your aim. If you are using a pistol like a 1911 semi-auto in Condition One (cocked-hammer), you may place your finger gently on the trigger at this time. Now you begin checking the alignment of your sights as you move the gun forward to the fully extended arms position.

Do not wait for the gun to be fully extended before focusing on your sights! This defeats the purpose of bringing the gun up into your line of sight close to your face. Use the time this technique gives you to get a head start on your aiming.

It's important for you to realize that, before your arms reach full extension, you have the ability to fire a coarsely aimed shot at a very close target, say within three yards, very quickly and with some notion of what your sight alignment is. By the time you reach full extension of the arms, you should already have a good sight picture and be able to fire the instant your arms cease motion on most shots that do not require extreme precision.

RE-HOLSTERING

Holstering the gun occurs as the reverse of the above motions. Think of it as running a movie backwards. The finger comes off the trigger as your two-handed grip moves the gun back towards your chest. The safety, if there is one, is reengaged and, as the gun rotates down towards the holster, the support forearm goes horizontal across your chest, its support hand parked at the "grab" position where it was first picked up by the gun. You should learn to re-holster without looking at the holster. Keep your eyes on the target (you may need to change your mind about re-holstering in a real-world situation!). You should also resist the urge to reach down and hold the holster with the support hand, as you will end up sweeping the gun muzzle across your support hand fingers.

Once the gun is holstered, run your fingers between the gun and your shirt, to make sure a fold of fabric has not been jammed down into the holster between the leather and gun. During this entire process, maintain your body's shooting posture (knees bent, fanny out, shoulders rounded towards the target), until the gun is holstered. Only once the gun is secured in the leather should you assume a normal posture.

CONCEALED GUNS

If you are going to carry concealed, you will need to clear your covering garment away from the handgun before you can grip the gun.

For sweeping aside an open jacket or coat, have the fingertips of your drawing hand raking across your shirt as you flip the garment open. Your hand should sweep the garment away and up to the pistol butt so you have clear access. Experiment with differing cover garments, as some will move aside in a satisfactory manner, while others will tend to cling to your shirt requiring a much slower "peeling" action.

For a non-opening, pullover type garment, grab the hem of the garment with both hands on either side of the hip holster and yank it far enough upwards to give several inches of clearance above the gun butt. It should go without saying that you do not want to be grabbing a handful of clothing wrapped around the gun butt.

***

The key to a quick draw is not forced speed, but, instead, a smooth, efficient movement without wasted motion. The technique is very simple, minimal, and direct, so resist the urge to make it more complicated than it needs to be. Slow makes smooth, and smooth makes fast.

CHAPTER 7

THE RELOAD

S ooner or later you will shoot your gun empty or almost
empty. There are two remedies to this, the speed load
and the tactical load.

The speed load is what its name implies; it's for when every
second counts, say, for instance, you are out of ammo yet still
engaged in a fight. A tactical reload is for when time is not of
the essence and you simply want or need to fully recharge your
weapon after the action is stopped momentarily or actually over.

*Slide locked back and
the gun empty! Time
for a speed load!*

It is always advisable to find hard (bulletproof) cover if you are in a fight, although that is not always possible at the first shots. But, by the time you need to reload, you should be behind something. Getting caught out in the open with an empty gun is bad news.

When performing the following techniques, keep your finger off the trigger and the muzzle pointed in a safe direction! It is common for thoughtless shooters to turn the pistol sideways and look at it, as though reading the writing on the side of the slide or barrel, when manipulating it for a reload. During practice, this results in pointing the muzzle at the fellow next to you on the firing line and, if in an actual gun fight, potentially at innocent bystanders. None of the techniques described next require holding the pistol sideways. They can and should all be performed keeping the muzzle downrange and your trigger finger off the trigger!

The support hand moves to the spare magazine (top photo), while the trigger hand shifts its grip to reach the magazine catch with thumb. Eject the magazine, letting it fall away freely, and grasp a new magazine using your fingertips. Note the gun stays just below face level — keep your eyes on the target!

SPEED LOADING THE SEMI-AUTO PISTOL

For a semi-auto pistol, you will want to bring the gun about halfway back to your body, just in front of your upper chest. You should be able to see your target just over the top of the gun. Keeping the muzzle pointed downrange, depress the magazine catch with your gun-hand thumb, while reaching for the spare magazine with your support hand. If your pistol has its catch located at the bottom of the butt, shift the support hand to the catch—you do not want to undo your trigger-hand's grip more than you have to—before reaching for your spare magazine. Whichever is your case, let the magazine fall to the ground. You can retrieve it after the reload has been completed and any situation has ended.

Bring up a fresh mag with a pointing index finger grip. Index the fresh magazine with your finger at the top rear corner, against the rear of the magazine well opening.

Seat the fresh magazine. Note the trigger finger is still clear of the trigger!

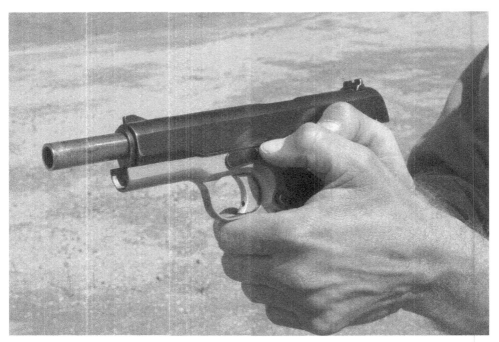

The support hand rotates to rejoin the firing grip, the support thumb disengaging the slide lock and releasing the slide to run forward into battery and chamber a round.

The slide closed in battery after a reload and the shooting grip resumed.

You should carry a spare magazine in a holder or pouch positioned so that the bullets face forwards. In this fashion, the natural grasping motion of the support hand brings up the magazine oriented in the manner necessary for proper insertion—no having to flip or spin the magazine around to get it right side up and bullets forward. It is much like drawing the gun; you need to grasp the magazine correctly the first time. When the magazine is fully in the hand and moving up towards the gun, have your forefinger lying straight along the leading edge of the magazine so as to help you "point" it into the magazine well.

Tilt the gun butt slightly towards the your hand as it comes up with the spare magazine. Place the top rear edge of the magazine against the rear face of the pistol magazine well opening, with the magazine bottom tilted somewhat rearwards

The old magazine falling, new magazine being drawn, and the gun angled to accept it.

A new magazine on the way towards the magazine well (left). Insert the new magazine. In this shooter's case, and while she's handling the gun safely, the gun muzzle is best kept more in line with the target.

relative to the gun, and "rock" or tilt the magazine straight as you press it home with a powerful shove. This two-part motion helps you locate the top of the magazine against the pistol correctly before giving it the shove inwards, thereby helping to eliminate fumbling or a thrust that misses the magazine well completely.

Do not be gentle when ramming home the magazine; the goal is to make sure the magazine is fully seated and the catch engaged. Rotate the pistol upright as the support hand reestablishes its proper grip. If you have shot the pistol completely empty and the slide is locked back, use the support-hand thumb to drop the slide lock lever as that hand moves into position. (If there is no itching need for absolute speed, give the magazine an extra smack on its base and then a tug on the toe of the magazine floorplate that sticks out the front of

You need to reload in a hurry? Let the old magazine fall free. Seconds count!

the magazine to make sure it is locked in place.) Then, switch your focus back to your front sight as you extend the pistol out to the normal firing position, and you are ready to go. Eventually, you want to be able to reload your gun without taking your eyes off your target.

THE TACTICAL RELOAD FOR SEMI-AUTO PISTOLS

The tactical load involves exchanging a partially loaded magazine for a full one, but also retaining the partially loaded unit on your person in case those last few rounds are needed later.

This is not a rushed maneuver. Unlike the speed load, you do not first drop the magazine that is in the gun; the first thing you do is to reach for the spare magazine. As you are bringing it up to the gun, maneuver the magazine in your hand so that its base is on the palm of your hand, its body is between the middle and ring fingers, and the curved front of the magazine body facing towards your fingers, not back towards your body. Bring this hand up under the butt of the pistol so that the web between forefinger and thumb is under the pistol butt, the spare magazine off to the outside of the gun, and then depress the magazine catch.

The semi-auto tactical load. Reach for spare mag with the pointing index finger grip. Note the trigger finger is clear of trigger, the gun is just below face level, and the eyes are on the target!

The spare magazine hand grip position (left). Note the magazine faces forward. Bring your support hand to the pistol and dump the old mag into your support hand between the thumb and index finger.

Insert the full spare magazine (left) without dropping the mag you've just ejected, and seat the full spare mag.

Drop the magazine from the gun butt into your palm so that it can be grasped between the thumb and forefinger, withdraw it from the gun completely, and then simply insert the spare magazine. Basically, all you're doing is exchanging magazines with the same hand at the same time.

Place the partially empty magazine in a pocket, not in your spare magazine carrier. You should reserve your carrier only for fully charged magazines. When your reload is complete, give a hard smack on the reloaded magazine's base and a little tug on the magazine floorplate toe to make sure it is locked in place.

RELOADING MODERN DOUBLE-ACTION REVOLVERS

There are numerous ways to recharge a revolver. You can reload with loose rounds, use the inline six-round Bianchi Speed Strips, speedloaders with handles that twists to let the rounds go (such as those from HKS), or, with certain revolvers, full- or half-moon clips that go into and stay with the handgun along with the cartridges.

A word of caution about reloading revolvers before we get to the techniques. You should never whip the cylinder open or closed unsupported via a flick of your wrist (like they did in old Hollywood gangster movies). This kind of rough treatment to a revolver will bend and warp the crane mechanism on which the cylinder pivots, resulting in a cylinder that no longer lines up true with the barrel. The methods outlined below avoid this.

Pocket the old mag. Now you are fully reloaded and have saved any leftover rounds in the partially depleted magazine.

THE REVOLVER SPEEDLOAD

I will cover the two main techniques that use the common varieties of speedloaders, since that is the most commonly used reloading device. I will also assume that the shooter is right-handed. Things get pretty complicated for a Southpaw wielding a gun built for a right-hander, but there is one method (a variant of the second technique I will cover) that will work fairly well for lefties.

From the two-handed revolver grip (left), perform the Method No. 1 speedload. Shift your support hand to cradle the gun underneath the trigger guard, while the trigger-hand thumb hits the cylinder release latch.

Open the cylinder, pushing it out with your support-hand middle and ring fingers, while continuing to maintain your trigger hand grip. The support-hand forefinger and pinky are vertical alongside the frame.

Holding the gun muzzle up with your support hand, eject the empties with a sharp slap on the ejector rod by the trigger hand.

Reach for your speedloader with your trigger hand. Move the speedloader's bullets forward to the revolver's open cylinder.

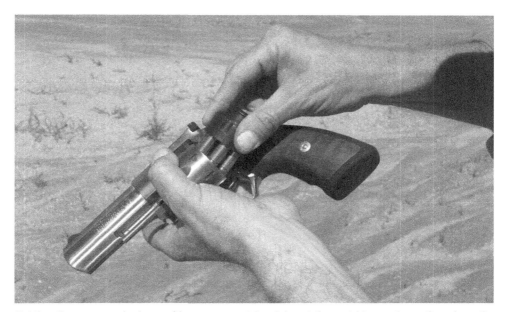

Holding the gun muzzle down with your support hand, insert the cartridges, release them from the speedloader, and drop or pocket the empty loader.

The cylinder fully loaded, your trigger hand goes to the gun's butt. Close the cylinder with your support hand and regain the firing grip with your trigger hand.

Method No. 1

The most commonly encountered technique for using speed-loaders is to first open the cylinder latch using the strong-hand thumb (again, assuming you are right-handed), while wrapping the support hand around the cylinder in such a way that the gun is transferred into that hand. The support hand moves under the gun and cradles the revolver such that the bottom of the trigger guard sits in the center of the palm; the forefinger and pinky

Revolver speedload Method No. 2: Shift your support grip to cradle the gun underneath the trigger guard, while the trigger-hand thumb hits the cylinder release latch, then open the cylinder while maintaining the grip on the gun with the trigger hand, just as in Method No. 1. The support-hand forefinger and pinky are vertical alongside frame, again, the same as in Method No. 1.

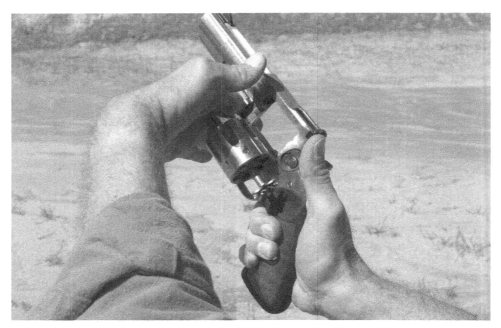

Maintaining the trigger hand firing grip and holding the gun muzzle up, the support hand leaves the cylinder and raps the ejector rod sharply.

finger are extended straight up with the forefinger alongside the right side of the forward part of the revolver frame (where the barrel screws in); and the pinky alongside the right rear part of the frame about in line with the hammer. The middle and ring fingers of the support hand, along with the thumb, capture the cylinder and swing it open, with the middle and ring fingers reaching through the frame opening (where the cylinder would be when closed), and maintaining a controlling grip on the cylinder against the thumb. This grip provides control of both the gun as a whole and the cylinder specifically. The strong hand leaves the butt of the gun as this support-hand grip is achieved.

At this point, the gun is rotated muzzle up and the empties are ejected via a sharp press down on the ejector rod. Activating the rod can be done with either the support hand thumb or the palm of the strong hand. The former method is faster and allows the strong hand to move towards the speedloader sooner. The latter method is more effective in getting all the empties out of the chambers. Whichever you use, watch for any empty case, especially the one closest to the gun frame, to hang up and not fall free.

Once the strong hand is freed of its duties, it reaches for the speedloader stored in a pouch or pocket, preferably on the

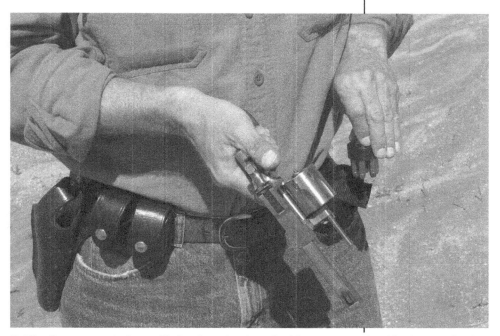

Holding the gun muzzle down with the trigger hand, reach with your support hand for the speedloader.

Holding the gun muzzle down with the trigger hand, insert cartridges with the support hand and release them from the speedloader.

With the cylinder fully loaded, drop or pocket the empty speedloader.

Close the cylinder ...

... and regain your support-hand grip.

To begin the tactical reload for a revolver, open the cylinder and, with the muzzle slightly down, extract the cartridges partially, about halfway out.

shooter's strong side. The gun muzzle is rotated to about a 45-degree downwards angle at the same time. Now, bring the loader into alignment with the chambers of the cylinder, slide the rounds in, and release them from the loader. Make sure they fall in, then move the loader away from the cylinder in a sideways motion. If it hangs up, it means you have one or more cartridges still partly in the speedloader. Do not withdraw the loader straight rearwards from the cylinder, as this can drag a round or two with it if they haven't fallen clear.

If you are in a big hurry, let the speedloader fall to the ground. The cradling support hand should move to close the cylinder at the same time the strong hand regains its firing grip on the gun butt (but being careful to keep the trigger finger outside the trigger guard). The shooter now regains the two-handed grip, if necessary, and is ready to go.

These motions of opening and transferring the gun to the support hand, then closing the gun and transferring it back to the strong hand, need to be performed smoothly, of course. Fortunately they are not difficult to master, and a little practice will go a long way towards this goal.

Let the extractor rod return to the forward position. Live rounds should slide in after it, while fired empty cases should stay in the extracted position.

Method No. 2

The second method is simpler than the first, in that the strong hand never leaves its firing grip and the support hand does all the work. However, it is also a bit slower.

In this method, the strong-hand thumb works the cylinder latch and the support hand reaches its fingers around the gun to open the cylinder as before. Here, though, the strong hand maintains its grip. The muzzle is elevated, and once the cylinder is opened, the support hand palm gives a sharp rap

**Remove the
empties.**

on the ejector rod, dumping the empties. The support hand
then reaches for a speedloader worn on the support side of
the body, as the firing hand lowers the gun muzzle to point
downwards. The loader is emptied into the cylinder as in the
previous method, with the support hand then closing the cylinder and regaining the two-hand grip if necessary.

THE LEFT-HANDED SPEED LOAD

Method No. 2 should work fairly well for a left-handed
shooter, if the shooter simply transfers the revolver from the
left hand into the right hand before performing the reload, then
transfers it back when done.

THE TACTICAL RELOAD FOR REVOLVERS

Probably the simplest way to do this is to start with the
Method No. 1 speedload described above. At the point where

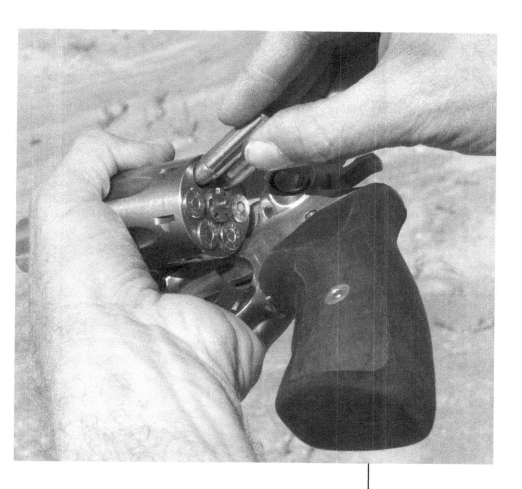

the cylinder is opened and the revolver grasped in the support hand, the muzzle is about 30 to 45 degrees below horizontal, and the support thumb depresses the ejector rod just enough to extract both the live and spent rounds about one-third of their length. Look at the primers of these rounds to see which ones have the dent from the firing pin. Those are the spent ones you want to pluck out. You can also gently ease the ejector rod forwards with the thumb, and the weight of the live rounds should let them slide back into their chambers; the spent cases will, for the most part ,stay in their partially extracted positions, making them easy to remove.

Replace the ones that need it with loose rounds. These can be carried loose in a belt pouch, in belt loops, or inserted one or two at a time from a Bianchi Speed Strip, which is a soft rubber strip into which cartridges are affixed by the case rims. Avoid dumping loose rounds into your pocket or purse. They rattle

Insert new live rounds and close the cylinder.

around, make noise, and get mixed up with loose change and other odds and ends, making it almost impossible to get at them.

If you have a belt or belt slide that holds individual rounds in loops, learn to pluck them out two at a time. Pull up on the bullets with your finger tips to raise the cartridges in their loops, getting your thumb behind the rims, then shift your fingertips to the case bodies to extract them completely. They will then be in your hand in perfect position to insert into the cylinder. This may seem slow and clumsy at first, but Jack Weaver, the Los Angeles County deputy who invented the Weaver stance, was able to fully reload his Smith & Wesson .38 duty revolver with two fast hand strokes grabbing three rounds each from belt loops, all

CHAPTER 8

CORRECTING MALFUNCTIONS

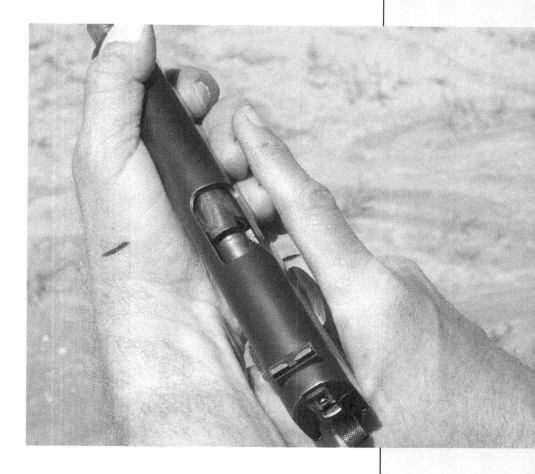

Having your gun jam is a nuisance, when you're at the range. Having it jam when you are fighting for your life can be fatal. Learning to quickly clear most common malfunctions may save your life someday. While the vast majority of us will never be in a gunfight, it is wise to ap-

A feeding jam. Note the cartridge is caught at an angle and holding back the slide.

proach the matter of malfunction clearances as though our lives depend upon them being speedy. Such an approach will ingrain the habits we'll need should the worst ever happen; otherwise, we tend to get into the habit of puttering around at the range, taking our own sweet time trying to figure out what is wrong and how to fix it. Heck, if nothing else, a fast clearance action will certainly impress your shooting buddies!

The methods that follow are designed for when you have the use of both hands. For a very comprehensive treatment of malfunction clearances using only the weak hand (which, of course, will also work with only the strong hand), I highly recommend obtaining Kelly McCann's excellent *Crucible* series of training videos.

When performing the following techniques, *keep your finger off the trigger and the gun's muzzle pointed in a safe direction!* It is common for inexperienced shooters to turn the pistol sideways and look at it when it malfunctions, just as they will when they need to reload. This, of course, results in pointing the muzzle at the fellow next to you on the firing line! If you insist on holding the pistol this way, turn your body to keep the muzzle pointed downrange! None of the techniques described here require holding the pistol sideways. They can and should all be performed keeping the muzzle downrange.

This slide is what is called "out of battery" (not closed all the way) by about ⅛-inch.

CORRECTING MALFUNCTIONS IN A SEMI-AUTO PISTOL

Semi-autos are very sensitive to ammunition. Different bullet shapes may hinder feeding of a cartridge into the chamber,

and underpowered ammunition may not have enough recoil to cycle the action completely, resulting in a failure to eject a spent case and chamber a fresh round. Failures to eject may also leave a spent case stuck in the ejection port, while weak magazine springs or dirty magazine interior walls may cause the attempted feeding of two rounds at once.

One reflex to keep in mind is to sharply smack the magazine bottom with the heel of the support hand, when seating the magazine in the pistol, as some malfunctions are caused by a

Use your support hand heel to smack to back of the slide.

magazine that is not fully inserted and locked into place. (In fact, while not always necessary, it's not a bad idea to preface the four clearance drills that follow with the words "magazine tap.") Another issue to keep in mind is that it is generally hard on a semi-auto pistol to let the slide slam forwards on an empty chamber when the slide had been locked open. Conversely, it is also unwise to ease the slide forward while first chambering a round of ammunition. When chambering a fresh round for the first time by hand, always let the slide slam forwards under its own spring pressure so that the gun goes fully into battery.

Feeding Failures

There are a few different types of feeding failures. First up, we may have a cartridge that hangs up on the feed ramp and fails to enter the chamber. The slide will be held most of the way open by the stuck round. Part of this problem that may need correcting may be that the rear end of the cartridge is still captured by the magazine feed lips. If this is the case, we cannot simply eject the offending round by racking the slide.

In this scenario, the support hand heel can deliver a blow to the back of the slide, forcing the nose of the bullet up the feed ramp and (we hope) fully into the chamber. If this fails, you'll need to lock the slide back and forcibly strip the magazine out of the pistol. The round hanging up will drag on the feed ramp, but should pry out of the magazine by your forced removal.

At this point, you'll have to inspect the magazine to make sure the next cartridge has positioned itself properly against the magazine feed lips and shake the pistol to make sure the stripped cartridge falls free, either out the bottom of the magazine well or out of the ejection port. If you are happy with the condition of the magazine, re-insert it and depress the slide lock lever, letting the slide run forwards freely. If you have any doubts about the magazine, pocket the bad magazine and go to your spare magazine—if you have one, and you should.

A second type of feeding failure results when round has left control of the magazine feed lips and its rim slid under the extractor hook, but the round has gotten stuck about halfway into the chamber at about a 30-degree angle. A sharp rap on the base of the magazine will often jar things enough to get the round unstuck and chambered. If not, we have three other options.

First, try slapping the back of the slide with the support hand heel to drive it into battery. This works a majority of the

> *One reflex to develop is to slap the back of the slide and/or the magazine bottom in the event of a misfeed.*

This magazine is not fully seated and will not feed the top round into the chamber.

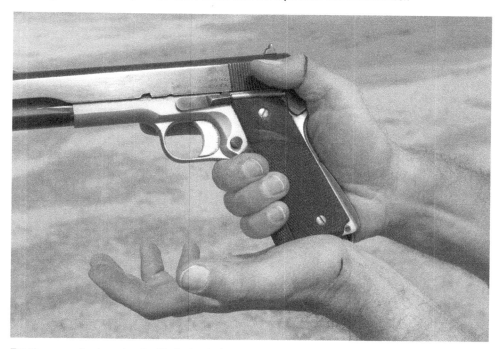

Tap the magazine base hard with the heel of the support hand.

Rack the slide to chamber a round.

Let the slide slam forward, chambering a round.

Regain your shooting grip.

time. If not, go to choice No. 2 and, with the support hand, ease the slide back about ¹/₈- to ¼-inch, then release it. This allows the head (rear) of the case to reposition itself properly by sliding up against the breech face of the slide and gets the cartridge straightened out, which allows it to go into the chamber. Third, and if all else fails, rack the slide sharply. Such a stuck cartridge likely has some of its rim engaged by the extractor hook, and racking the slide will extract and eject the troublesome round before chambering the next in line.

In a third type of feeding failure, we may have a round chambered, but the slide doesn't return quite all the way forward, usually by a distance of less than ¼-inch. The gun will not fire in this mode; the hammer will not drop at the trigger pull.

Now, the first thought is to smack the back of the slide with the support hand. But this particular feeding issue is a bit tricky because, if the problem is caused by an oversized or otherwise deformed round, it is already jammed in as far as it wants to go and a hard slap on the back of the slide will only jam it in there even tighter, perhaps still not far enough to go into battery (which will allow the gun to fire) and perhaps so tight that you will be unable to rack the slide in the event the slap doesn't work. Therefore, the safest procedure is to lightly nudge the back of the slide with the heel of the support hand and, if that doesn't cause it to go all the way forwards, then sharply rack the slide to eject the troublesome round and chamber a new one. Note that considerable force might be necessary to pull back the slide and eject the round if it's a deformed cartridge that's jammed in the chamber. If time is of the essence, the fastest way to rectify this problem is to skip the nudge and just rack the slide.

Still another feeding problem can be encountered. In this instance, the gun will appear to have cycled normally, but, when you pull the trigger, all you hear is a click instead of a bang. This is another tricky situation, because there are three potential causes.

First, there's the possibility that there's been a failure to cycle the action far enough to extract and eject the empty case and chamber a fresh round. This is most often caused, especially with inexperienced shooters, by a weak grip. It can also be the result of underpowered ammunition. Second, it can be the result of a failure to fully seat the magazine, in which case the top round rides too low to be picked up by the slide. When this happens, you get an empty chamber after the ejection of the last fired case. Finally, the problem can be an instance of a cartridge without powder in it.

A stovepiped case. Note that the next round is attempting to chamber.

The stovepipe from the shooter's perspective.

1) Starting the stovepipe wipe with the support hand.

2) Wiping the case away with a rearward stroke of the support hand. Note the empty case spinning just below the support hand.

3) The support hand snaps forward to the pistol.

4) The support hand regains its shooting grip.

In this third case, we have a serious safety issue. While you won't hear a bang, you also won't hear a click. It'll be somewhere in-between, and it's the sound of the primer discharging. You must understand that a primer discharge alone it is powerful enough to drive the bullet out of the case and partway down the barrel—having a bullet stuck in the bore while firing another round behind it is a prescription for your gun blowing up in your hand like a grenade.

> *Hear something between a click and a bang? That's the primer discharging behind a powderless cartridge–and you could have a serious safety issue.*

If you suspect you've fired a powderless case, you must stop and check for an obstructed bore. The simplest way to do this is to drop the magazine out of the pistol, lock open the pistol, and slide a slim rod down the bore from the muzzle end, seeing if it stops partway down or comes all the way through to the rear of the chamber. For a larger-bore pistol like a .45, a pencil or slim pen works. Something slimmer will be necessary for smaller calibers. If you don't have anything to slide down the bore, insert your fingertip into the ejection port against the breechface with the fingernail facing the chamber and look down the muzzle. If there is any light available from an empty bore, it should be visible reflecting off your fingernail.

The Stovepipe

Another kind of malfunction occurs when the spent case does not fully leave the gun and is caught by the slide as it is closing on the next round. The case will be sticking up out of the ejection port in a vertical or near-vertical position, thereby preventing the slide from closing. This is called a "stovepipe" and is a very obvious problem to see.

The cure for this is a quick sweep of the forefinger-side edge of the support hand over the top of the slide, knocking the stovepipe out of the port and letting the slide close. There should be a fresh round picked up by the slide on its way into the chamber in this situation, but, if there isn't, you may find yourself doing a tap-rack-ready drill, if you get a "click" after you pull the trigger.

A variation of the stovepipe is a case caught in the horizontal position between the breechface and the rear face of the barrel, holding the slide almost all the way open. These require a racking of the slide, accompanied by a rolling of the pistol to the right side, to allow the case to fall out of the ejection port. Rarely, some cases stuck in this manner may require being plucked out with the fingers, after you lock the slide back.

The dreaded double feed, a round in the chamber and another trying to chamber right behind it.

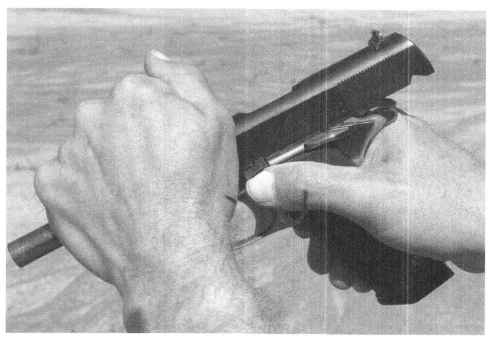

Lock back the slide to remove the recoil spring pressure against the cartridge.

Strip out your magazine and place it under your trigger hand pinky finger.

Rack the slide two or three times to clear the chamber.

Release the slide to come forward on its own power. Don't ride it forward with your hand.

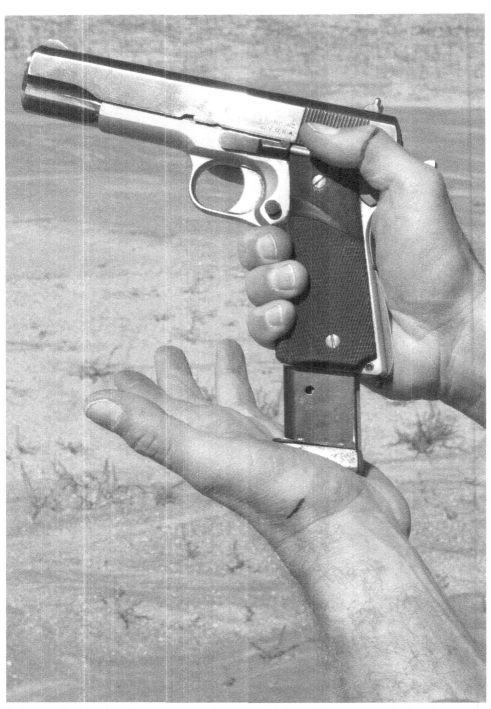

Reload, preferably with a fresh magazine, since you don't know if the magazine that was in the gun was the originator of the double feed.

Rack the slide again to chamber a round.

Release the slide again.

*Regain your firing grip
and resume business.*

The Double-Feed Malfunction

This is the toughest problem to fix. It is also the most time-consuming. In fact, it will seem like an eternity, if you are doing it against the clock or while under fire.

What you will see when a double feed happens is the slide being held almost fully open. When you look in the ejection port, you'll see the top round in the magazine being pushed up by the slide and against another round already in the chamber. There are six distinct steps involved to fix it and, while it takes a lot of practice, it can be done in four or five seconds. (As a side note, in a fight situation, this is where you will really appreciate the value of good cover.)

A double feed is caused when the slide tries to feed a round up from the magazine, but the chamber is already occupied by another round or spent case. The spring pressure on the slide causes the bullet of the round coming up from the magazine to bind tightly against the rear face of the case already in the chamber. When this happens, your gun comes to a screeching halt. The problem was caused either by an extraction failure of the case in the chamber (due to a broken extractor or a badly stuck case), or by the magazine being dirty inside or having a weak spring.

In the case of a weak spring or dirty magazine, as the slide retracts to bring the fired case out of the chamber, the bottom of the slide clears the top of the magazine as the slide goes rearwards. Since, when it's forward, the bottom of the slide always depresses the top cartridge of the magazine slightly, this top round is now pushed up slightly by the magazine spring. It is this motion that is critical. If the magazine spring is strong and the movement of its coils are not impeded by dirt inside the magazine body, the top round will be quickly captured by the magazine feed lips and held in place during the violent rearwards recoil motion of the gun. It will then be scooped up by the slide in its forward stroke. This operation fails when the upward motion of the top round in the magazine is slow. If it is slow, the violent rearwards motion of the gun in recoil can cause the top round to slip forward out of the magazine before the magazine spring pressure can bind that round against the feed lips. Since the chamber has just been vacated by the extracted case, and the whole gun, including the feed ramp and chamber, is still in rearwards recoil motion, the top round from the magazine, now loose, simply bounces up the feed ramp and into the chamber as the slide reaches the end of its rearwards motion.

The press check. Remove the magazine and place it under your trigger hand pinky.

Grip the slide just behind muzzle with your support-hand fingers and retract it about a ½-inch.

Two things happen next. First, the slide starts forward again, and the next round of the magazine is pushed up to the top position by the magazine spring. As the slide starts forward, it scoops up this next round from the magazine, which then jams up against the rear of the round that just found its way into the chamber. Presto, a double feed.

The thing to remember about clearing the double feed is that the recoil spring pressure pushing forward on the slide binds up the whole works, and that pressure must be relieved by locking the slide to the rear before any other remedial action can be taken. Once you've done that, the next steps are:

1) Strip the magazine out of the gun and store it under the pinky finger of the strong hand.
2) Rack the slide two or three times to clear the chamber of whatever is in it.

3) Reload, preferably with your spare magazine, since the original problem may have been magazine-caused.

4) Rack the slide again to chamber the top round from the new magazine.

Let's look at some of these steps closely.

First, don't forget to lock the slide back as the first operation you do after identifying the double feed. Fail to do this, and you won't get the magazine to budge.

When you get to the next step, stripping out the magazine, expect that this action will usually cause the top round to pop out of the magazine and fall out of the magazine well. Watch for it to make sure it clears the gun completely.

On step No. 2, let the slide slam shut (do not retard it's movement forward), so as to facilitate speed of the operation and to make sure the extractor hook snaps over the rim of the case in the chamber. And don't forget step No. 4, racking the slide after inserting the new magazine—remember, you inserted the magazine under a slide that is now closed on an empty chamber (you just emptied it in step No. 2).

Look into the ejection port to see if a round is chambered.

THE PRESS CHECK

The press check is how you determine whether your gun is fully loaded or not. To begin the press check, with the gun held in your strong-hand firing grip (finger off the trigger, of course), remove the magazine with your support hand, check its load, and then clasp it under your strong-hand pinky finger. Next, reach your support hand under (not in front of!) the muzzle and grasp the end of the slide on either side of the front sight. (If you have a 1911-type auto in cocked-and-locked mode, you'll need to depress the thumb safety first.) Press rearwards firmly to open the slide about a ½-inch or so and look into the top of the ejection port. If there is a cartridge in the chamber, you will see it partially extracted from the chamber.

> Are you fully loaded, chamber and magazine? If you are not fully aware of the condition of your gun, you really shouldn't be carrying one.

Now you know what is in the magazine and what is in the chamber. Let the slide run forward, put on the safety if applicable, and re-insert the magazine with a firm shove, followed by a sharp rap with the heel of the hand and a tug on the floorplate toe. This press-check motion should be a frequent habit when handling and shooting semi-auto pistols. If you are not fully aware of the condition of your gun, you really shouldn't be carrying one.

A word about malfunctioning semi-autos. There are many reasons for the various malfunctions described above. The most common is when a certain type of pistol and a certain shape of bullet disagree with each other. You must experiment with different types of ammunition to find what your gun likes. Do not trust any ammunition that you have not fired through your pistol at least 100 times (and more is certainly better). Some pistols may have manufacturing quality control problems, such as rough surfaces or sharp edges along the cartridge feed path, or perhaps the magazine isn't made to specification. Pay close attention to how your pistol works with different ammo and magazines. Too, you should mark your magazines so you can tell which ones are which if you notice periodic malfunctions. And, if your pistol malfunctions regularly with different brands of ammo and different magazines, it may need the attention of a gunsmith. Wring out your pistol well and get intimately familiar with it—you ought not to trust your life to it otherwise!

Finally, if you grip the gun weakly and with a loose wrist that allows excess muzzle flip in recoil, this has the effect of reducing the power and speed with which the slide travels rearward against the frame. This can weaken the force available for empty case extraction from the chamber and ejection from the port in the slide, and may also cause the slide to not travel far enough rearward to pick up the next cartridge from the top of the magazine before it returns forward into battery. Don't "limp wrist" your pistol.

CORRECTING MALFUNCTIONS IN A REVOLVERS

Being manually operated, revolvers do not share quite the same kinds of malfunctions as autoloaders, but there are some ammunition-related issues that can cause you a headache, as well as those that result from cleanliness issues.

Pulled Bullets

The recoil from firing a revolver puts some inertial stress on the bullets of the cartridges in their chambers. Unlike a semi-auto pistol's rounds in their magazine, which simply thrust up against the front wall of the magazine under recoil, cartridges in a revolver are held by their rims (usually) and have no forward barrier against which the bullet noses can come to rest. Therefore, a cartridge case with a weak or insufficient crimp on its bullet may allow that bullet to move forward in its casing under the forces of recoil.

If such a movement lets the nose of the bullet extend forward beyond the front face of the cylinder, this bullet will bind against the rear of the barrel or the side of the frame, as the cylinder tries to revolve. This pretty well stops the rotation of the cylinder dead in its tracks.

The remedy is to open the gun and pluck out the offending cartridge, reload with another round if available, and manually index the cylinder so that the next good cartridge is just before the barrel when the cylinder closes. It is a good idea to look at the front of the cylinder (while it's open!) to ascertain whether or not there are any other such defective rounds. A last note: if such rounds are handloaded, they need to have a stronger crimp of the case mouth applied onto the bullet.

Flowed Primer Cups

Once upon I time I saw a brand-new Smith & Wesson Model 19 .357 Magnum revolver, firing factory Remington .357 Magnum ammunition, locked up tight. The cylinder could be neither rotated nor opened. Close inspection revealed some sort of obstruction between the rear of the fired cartridge case still in the firing position (in line with the barrel) and the face of the frame opening, right about where the firing pin comes forward.

It turned out that some of the metal of the primer cup had, under the pressure of firing, flowed back slightly into the firing pin hole. That bit of metal had just enough grip to prevent the cylinder from moving.

The cure was to hold open the cylinder release while applying a sharp blow from a wooden or plastic mallet to the right side of the cylinder, shearing away the extruded primer cup metal and opening the cylinder. Should this become your problem, carefully clean out any remaining metal shavings from the firing pin hole in the face of the frame opening and check to be sure the firing pin protrudes correctly when the hammer is in the firing (cocked) position.

Backed-Out Extractor Rod

A similar locking-up effect can be caused by the extractor rod, protruding from the front of the cylinder, unscrewing itself slightly. This causes it to bind against the spring-loaded catch under the barrel that captures the front end of the extractor rod when the cylinder is closed.

The cure for this is to take a small needle-nose pliers and gently (so as not to mar the rod surface) rotate it back to its normal position. The direction in which to turn it is a good question, as different makers may have right or left threads on their products, and some, as it is with my Ruger GP100, do not rotate at all (which should keep you from having this malfunction, at least!).

Fouling Under the Extractor Star

If dirt, soot, or loose, unburned powder grains accumulate underneath the cartridge extractor, it will not seat fully into its recess in the rear face of the cylinder. This makes it protrude slightly to the rear, and it can bind against the rear face of the frame opening. This makes the gun difficult to close and open, and also makes it difficult for the cylinder to turn.

The solution is to thoroughly clean the inside face of the extractor star and the inside its cylinder recess, and keep these areas clean. A toothbrush works well for this chore.

Case Rim Slipping Past the Extractor

This happens when the rim of a fired case has the extractor star slip past it. The solution, while keeping the extractor fully extended rearwards, is to firmly grasp the head of the offending case, pull it out until its head comes back against the extractor, and simply pry it out sideways with a healthy tug. Otherwise, it will prevent the extractor star from retracting properly, putting your gun completely out of action.

Failure of a Round to Fire

If you are on the range practicing, it is wise to halt your shooting, stay on the line with the muzzle pointed downrange, and wait 30 seconds to see if there will be a delayed firing of the

cartridge, something known as a "hang fire." Next, attempt to determine, as described in the semi-auto section, if a powderless cartridge has had its primer launch the bullet partway down the barrel, creating an obstruction. You absolutely do not want to fire another shot if the inside of the barrel is obstructed!

Keep the area under the extractor star clean of dirt and powder fouling.

CONDITION CHECK

This serves the same purpose as the press-check in a semi-auto pistol. While gripping the revolver with the strong hand in a proper firing grip (finger off the trigger, of course), cradle the support hand under the revolver so that the cylinder can be gripped between thumb and fingers. With the firing hand thumb, open the cylinder catch, ease the cylinder open with the support hand fingers, and visually inspect the chambers for cartridges. Next, inspect the primers to see how many are fired. In the dark, you can disengage the grip of the support hand to run your fingertip around the chambers to check for cartridges, although it will be almost impossible to feel whether the primers are indented. If in doubt, reload the whole cylinder.

CHAPTER 9

HITTING FASTER

"If you can't perform the basics slow-firing on a single target, you can't get to the fancier stuff. Crawl, walk, run."

L et's regroup for a second and sum what we've learned in the prior chapters.

1) Accurate pistol shooting is based on having trained our hands to properly perform alignment of the gun with the target, and we confirm this alignment with our eyes and mind through the flash sight picture.

2) It is the eyes that teach the hands to bring the gun to eye level and point to where the eyes are looking, and it takes a lot of training to make this happen.

3) When you have accomplished No. 2, the hands perform correctly by themselves, and the eyes merely verify what the hands have already done. This is a form of trained, reflexive, eye-level point shooting that is visually checked and mentally approved before the trigger is pulled. It is vitally important that you understand and train to this concept!

So far we have covered safe gun handling, mindset, basic pistol marksmanship, the draw from a belt holster, reloading, and malfunction clearances. These form the bread and butter foundations of good handgun skills.

Going forward, let's agree upon the basic notion that you have to learn to walk before you can learn to run. It is vitally important to understand that if you can't perform the basics of hand/gun/target alignment, flash sight picture verification, trigger control, and accuracy on a single target with slow fire, you can't do anything fancier, since the performing the fancier things requires at least the same skill set as do the basics. Please make sure you practice diligently enough to shoot small groups in a methodical and deliberate manner at ranges out to about 15 yards (or even more), with the sights being brought to the target by the hands first, clearly seeing your sight picture every shot, working to develop consistently proper trigger management, and breaking yourself of any flinching through the compressed surprise break, before charging ahead with the following. Getting too far ahead of your skill set will only breed frustration.

But what about learning to shoot faster? What about engaging multiple targets? What about moving targets and shooting while you're on the move? How do we do that, and what kind of drills can we practice to gain these skills?

When we get into the topic of shooting faster, what we really want is to *hit* faster. This, in turn, brings up the question of how much accuracy we need—or, how much inaccuracy we can get away with—for a given target size and distance.

> *When we talk about shooting faster, what we really mean is hitting faster.*

THE ACCEPTABLE SIGHT PICTURE

While learning the basic marksmanship skills, we want to work with a small area or point at which to aim. This kind of focus forces us to perfect our skills, even knowing that, in the practical sense for hunting or self-defense, we usually have a desirable hit zone or area quite a bit larger than a small point with which to work. So, bear in mind that, while we don't want this larger target area to allow us to let us get sloppy, we do have some degree of room in which to place our hits.

On a human adversary, a 10-inch circle or a six-inch by 12-inch vertical rectangle centered in the upper chest is usually acknowledged as a workable target zone. You also may have heard of the "sniper triangle," the area from nipple to nipple, and up to the base of the throat at the top of the breastbone. (As an aside, for a game animal, the circle holds true, though usually in the lower forward area of the chest, with the size of the zone commensurate to the size of the animal.)

If we're just fooling around on the range or going for the X-ring in bull's-eye competition, we can take our time. But, if we want to get the best speed while still keeping our hits in the area we want, it is okay to use up the entire permissible target area if it helps us gain speed, and as long as we maintain accuracy-based control. This is done through recognizing that, while a sight picture may not be perfect, it is good enough to get a hit in the area we want. This can only be learned through shooting a lot of rounds at different distances with less than perfect sight pictures, and comparing your remembered call for that shot to its placement on the target. (You are calling each shot, aren't you?)

One more topic that will need consideration and development is the mental aspect of shooting. The physical act of firing a shot is quite simple. The mental aspect of this is simple, too, but it is often difficult for us to allow this to be so. Quite a bit goes on in the human mind that tends to distract from and clutter this process. The ability to clear the mind, so as to divorce your conscious thoughts, fears, desires, and other emotions from what you're doing, is quite difficult to manage, but necessary to reach full performance potential. Think of more advanced performance as being enabled not by doing more, but by doing less, by stripping away the mental encumbrances that trip up our performances and by reducing the act to its barest essentials. Good pistol shooting at high speed is really a minimalist activity.

Couch potatoes beware! The techniques related in the rest of this chapter cannot be learned without frequent, regular, intense, thoughtful, and perfect dry-fire and live-fire practice! If you are looking for some super-secret technique as a short-cut for jumping to the next level of high-speed performance, understand that no such thing exists. There just ain't no short cut here!

INCREASING YOUR HIT SPEED

Notice the subhead here says hit speed and not firing speed. Shooting faster and missing only gets you more practice in reloading. In a lethal confrontation, that kind of approach can be suicidal. What we want is the ability to speed the slow-fire process while keeping our accuracy within the boundaries of the target size and distance. We do not leave anything out of the slow-fire process. Simply, we take the process and speed it up.

Two things are imperative for faster hitting: a reflexive mental and optical lock on the front sight that becomes subconscious; and a trigger press that is quick, does not disturb the gun, and also becomes subconscious. Remember, the flash sight picture is the boss of the trigger finger, and you must be totally and constantly aware of the quality of your sight picture over tiny fractions of a second. You must also teach your trigger finger a smooth, correct, reflexive, and subconscious motion based on an acceptable sight picture that occurs at high speed, but without disturbing your aim. Without these elements, you will be wasting a lot of ammo.

Reaching the next level of performance requires that the shooter grow from using conscious thought about shooting procedures to having these procedures ingrained in the subconscious mind, i.e., conscious thought is will no longer be a necessity to the required performance level. This allows the processes involved to move along at a much higher rate of speed through subconscious reflexes. So, how do we get there? High repetition correctly performed with a clear, unbiased, unforced, and relaxed mind will allow the best progression to faster speeds. In other words, don't *think* about shooting fast, don't *try* to shoot fast, just clear your mind and shoot—a lot.

> You must remember that it is a good sight picture that triggers the process of shooting. It is not a blind, reflexive jerk of the trigger that gets the job done.

The primary method we use to gain speed is simple repetition—lots and lots of practice, both dry- and live-fire. Forced physical speed of motion is usually a mistake. Smoothness and economy of motion is preferred. Through repetition, we gain both familiarity with the physical and mental acts of firing a shot and a mental/physical/neural programming process, which enables the mind to *perceive* more quickly and, thus, the body to *act* more quickly. This process will be familiar to anyone who has studied sports psychology and the process of human performance training. Aiding and abetting this process is the act of shedding all the mental and emotional baggage as described previously (and why the study of the Zen concept of "no mind" is pursued by serious martial artists). These are the techniques of high-performing athletes and martial artists, and they work the same way for shooting.

What the shooter will experience is faster presentation of the gun to the aiming position, increased perfection of the alignment of the gun with the target via the presentation, increased speed acquiring and judging the sight picture (the flash sight picture), and, finally, a trigger pull that is purely subconscious reflex. The instant the brain verifies the sight picture as being adequate for a hit, it directs a subconscious trigger pull far faster than the conscious mind can deliver. You will experience seeing your correct sight picture, and about the time your conscious mind starts to say to itself "that looks good, I can press the trigger," the gun will fire before your mind gets past the "that."

The first time this happens, it will startle you. You might even think you had some sort of accidental discharge. But, if you think about what your eye was seeing when the gun fired and realize it was a good sight picture, you will understand that you just experienced your first subconscious trigger reflex. When this happens consistently and automatically, it opens the door to speed shooting. *What is important to remember is that it is the good sight picture that triggers the process.* It is not a blind, reflexive jerk on the trigger, but rather the speeding up

of the correct and complete process rising from the conscious action level to the subconscious reflex level. Needless to say, it takes thousands of repetitions to gain this kind of proficiency.

This usually is first achieved when you have either presented the pistol accurately and instantly perceived a correct flash sight picture, or already fired one shot at a fairly close target with your eyes catching both the upward lift of the front sight in recoil and its recovery back to the same good sight picture that you used to fire the first shot. The brain recognizes this (our old friend the flash sight picture), in as little as $1/100$-second and triggers off a follow-up shot subconsciously, the time between

Note the empty case only a short distance above the pistol muzzle, yet the gun is already recovered from recoil and back on target.

shots seeming almost non-existent, but actually measuring somewhere around a quarter to a fifth of a second (as timed with an electronic shot timer—Google it).

What happens if you have a bad sight picture after your first shot? If you fire, you'll produce a bad hit, unless you put the brakes on and first correct your sight picture. If you find yourself not breaking the second shot upon seeing a too-incorrect sight picture, it is likely your subconscious mind balking at firing specifically *because* the sight picture is bad. This is sometimes called "trigger block." This, too, can be disconcerting, since your conscious mind may be in such a hurry-up mode that you will be stumped by the refusal of your trigger finger to budge. Really, this can happen! If it does, take a good conscious look at your sight picture, make any necessary correction, and resume shooting. Better to hesitate a tiny fraction of a second to correct a bad sight picture than to waste a shot.

MEASURING SPEED AND UNDERSTANDING POTENTIAL

It is important to understand that subconscious perception of a poor sight picture after recoil recovery, and its correction, can be accomplished in less than a tenth of second with intense practice. By my experience with an electronic shot timer, about $3/100$- to $4/100$-second when I am on top of my game (and I shoot only at about a 65-percent (B Class) comparative skill to a top-level Grand Master competitive practical shooter in the United States Practical Shooting Association). To be clear, this is not first shot to second shot time. It is the time difference between one shot pair fired at the same target (called a "split") and having a good automatic sight picture recovery after recoil from the first shot, versus a split with faulty sight alignment after the first shot that requires some degree of correction before firing the second shot.

Shot timers can teach you much. Put one on your needed-gear list; most run a little over $100. By realizing this level of performance is possible, you will drive on to this objective and not be tempted to settle for less. Those who say you can't shoot fast with sights and have perception and control of the process don't know what they're talking about (probably because they have not reached this level of performance and understanding). This is one of the factors that fuels that annoying and mostly irrelevant debate between sighted and point shooting you've probably seen raging on the Internet or heard on the firing line at your local range (more on that below).

CONTROL

For now, you should always verify your sight picture before the shot is released. This is how you maintain accuracy control over your speed. Otherwise, the wheels come off. Know, too, that the fastest speed at which you can verify your flash sight picture is the fastest speed at which you should be shooting. This is what ingrains correct and accurate performance and teaches the hands to bring the gun into alignment with where your eyes are looking. It is the underlying foundation for fast accurate shooting using your sights.

Types of Shot Splits at the Same Target

In the development and teaching of Jeff Cooper's Modern Technique of the Pistol, the varying types of faster shooting are defined by how the sight picture is used to control the shooting tempo. In the book of the same name, Gregory Morrison, a one-time instructor at Gunsite Academy under Cooper, details how a pair of shots is executed in what is called a "controlled pair." The sequence is:

1) Sight picture
2) Go or make a correction
3) Trigger press
4) Recoil
5) Reacquire the sight picture
6) Go or make a correction
7) Trigger press

In this sequence, each shot is fired after seeing and evaluating a flash sight picture, which may include correcting a poor sight picture. This is the most precise and the slowest tempo.

A shot pair executed following this sequence but without pausing to make a sight picture correction after recoil from the first shot is called a "dedicated pair." In this manner, the second sight picture is dedicated to the alignment in which the gun recovers from recoil. The speed of the second shot in a dedicated pair sequence is slightly greater than that of the second shot of a controlled pair, but the second shot accuracy of a dedicated pair may suffer if the gun comes down slightly out of alignment. Still, for gaining speed on a closer target it may still suffice.

A shot executed as "sight picture/go-or-correct/press/recoil/press" is called a "hammer." Here, the sight picture after the recoil of the first shot may not even be seen; basically, you are firing two quick shots off of one sight picture. This is very fast, but, again, accuracy of the second shot may suffer if your hands are not well enough trained in alignment. Also, when one's hands are trained well enough in muscle memory to automatically align the handgun accurately on the target (the necessary goal of your draw/presentation practice!) the first shot presentation sight picture may be not even be focused on by the eyes. Instead, the brain recognizes that the position of the blurry gun along eyesight line and the feel in the hands/arms is enough to hit the target somewhere in its central zone, and, so, your brain may subconsciously trigger the shot even without flash sight picture verification. This is useful at very close ranges, where precision isn't necessary, but speed is of the essence. Remember that instant accuracy of alignment must eventually come from proper aiming with the hands, which only comes from frequent and regular perfect practice. Practice perfectly, constantly! (Nag, nag.)

From my own experience, the above descriptions are useful when learning the reflexes required for faster shooting. I think these descriptions serve to tell you what type of shooting you are executing and help you to understand just what processes are happening. I believe that a beginner should attempt to shoot nothing but controlled pairs at first. As you attempt to speed up, you may find your trigger finger outpaces your eye/mind

An electronic shot timer, showing total time to the second, final shot, the split time between the first and second shot, and (not quite visible), time to the first shot after the buzzer was initiated.

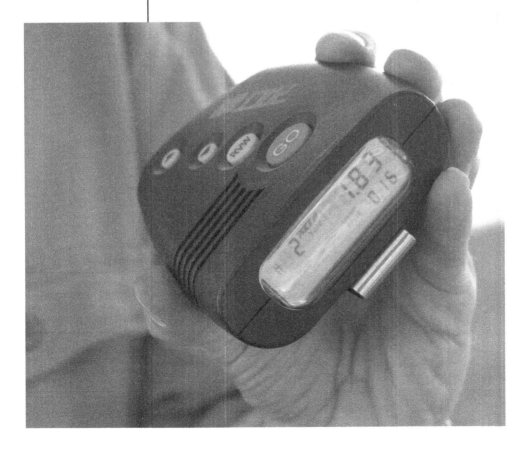

process, so that the second shot "gets away" from you. When that happens, instead of the intended controlled pair, you've shot a dedicated pair (or a hammer instead of a dedicated pair). This will be somewhat accidental at first, but, if your grip is correct, the gun will recover to a very good sight picture, the hits ought to be good enough, and you will have effected a proper occurrence of the technique, though performed unintentionally.

When this unexpected occurrence happens, focus on immediately remembering what you saw in the sight picture for that shot and check the accuracy of the shot that got away. This will teach you whether you just did some unintended variation correctly (or not), and which variation it was. The trick is not to let the speeding-up process get out of control and produce poor shooting. With experience, you will recognize that an imperfect sight picture may still be good enough to get the required hits, so that a controlled pair morphs into a dedicated pair and a dedicated pair can become a hammer.

Once your reflexes of seeing, deciding, and triggering are sufficiently developed in the subconscious mode, you will learn and develop through controlled pair/dedicated pair/hammer and then back to a point of doing almost all your shooting in the controlled pair variety, but now executable at very high speeds at close to moderate distances (to 15 yards), and only slightly slower at longer ranges. How? Your perception abilities will speed up so that the second shot of a dedicated pair becomes more quickly realized and corrected, turning into a controlled pair without slowing down. Your controlled pair perception speed then starts to match the speed of what used to be your dedicated pair. Ditto the process of turning a hammer into a dedicated pair without slowing it down. As skills, experience, and perception build, you will also recognize what is an acceptable sight picture for a given shot and shoot with the corresponding technique to produce the speed and accuracy combination desired. For a seasoned and well-trained shot, the process happens automatically—subconsciously! As your shooting evolves, the dedicated pair and hammer will simply begin to happen at the very close targets.

The key for the shooter in the learning process is to use accuracy as the controlling factor for developing speed and technique. Whatever else happens, you must get consistent hits. Fast misses solve nothing, and you can't miss fast enough to catch up.

> *The trick is not to let the speeding-up process get out of control and produce bad shooting.*

The timer has a delayed start option, so you can clip it on your belt and time your training drills without needing another warm body.

CONCENTRATION

Okay, having read this far, how great a level of concentration do you think will be required to achieve all this? You need continuous visual concentration on the front sight without blinking through a shot string, and mental concentration on what the front sight is doing to provide the feedback needed by the mind to accurately control the hands and trigger finger at speeds faster than the eye blinks.

A good drill for developing speed of recoil recovery, sight picture re-acquisition, and subconscious reflexive trigger management is the "Bill Drill." Set up a target at seven yards. It can be a standard IPSC or IDPA target, or perhaps just an eight-inch bull's-eye target such as a 100-yard smallbore rifle target or, if you are broke like me, a paper plate. Your aiming point will be in the center of the A-zone or bull's-eye.

In this drill, you'll fire six shots, the first shot starting from the holster. With each shot, you want to keep your eyes on the sights while the gun is in recoil and witness the entire cycle of front sight motion up and down without blinking. Concentrate! When it comes back down, instantly verify the sight picture, correct if necessary, and shoot again. Try to keep all your shots in the target zone, and try to see the full cycle of gun motion. With enough practice at this, you will see your gun snap down after recoil as fast as it went up, and you will see the reformation of your sight picture as it happens. This will lead to the desired subconscious trigger reflex. When your front sight comes down from recoil to a perceived perfect sight picture, the gun should fire *instantly*.

This should look like a movie of your front sight bobbing up and down at high speed and without the sight hesitating at the on-target position. If the sight recovers from recoil incorrectly, learn to see this and correct it before triggering the next shot. Top competitive IPSC shooters of the Grand Master or Master rank can get six A-zone hits in the vicinity of two seconds, holster draw included!

Getting a fast split time—the time between two shots to the same aim point on the same target—is nice to have, but its application is limited to hammering a single target with multiple rounds. This has some use if you are required to do this in a competition or are faced with a single opponent in a lethal confrontation. And, yes, it's fun to empty a magazine this way. But its true value lies in creating the ability to rapidly present the gun with a good physical alignment index, instantly see your sight picture, instantly decide if the sight picture is good or requires correction, instantly perform a needed correction, instantly press off the shot, and instantly see and gauge your post-recoil sight picture, all at a phenomenal speed and while not missing. In other words, obtaining fast split times without misses means you've ingrained your processes from the conscious to the subconscious. This is expert-level shooting.

Running timed draw-and-shoot-twice drills. One empty case is visible against the sky, the other is just below and right of it at the edge of the skyline.

POINT SHOOTING

After all my emphasis on focusing on the front sight, I have been loathe to even include this subject at risk of having you jump off the track of proper reflexive sight use. But understanding point shooting is important and does have its place in your battery of shooting skills. That said, I think you will be best served by really ingraining your sighted shooting before spending too much energy on the following.

First of all, what is point shooting? At its simplest, it is shooting without first referencing a clear sight picture, most likely to gain speed in shooting a lethal adversary who is so close that he not only presents split-second, imminent danger to you, and also so close that such an adversary does not require precisely aimed fire to be hit. The idea here is that bringing the handgun up to eye level is not required (from an accuracy standpoint) and, more importantly, will cost more time than you have.

Point shooting is usually done from below eyesight level, using an alignment achieved with both hands and body. It also usually involves the gun hand being kept close in to the body, to keep your enemy from grabbing or deflecting it. The closer your enemy, the closer your gun is kept to your body.

Point shooting is a controversial subject among both shooters and trainers. Basically, there's the "always use sighted fire because you'll miss otherwise" crowd versus the "never use the sights because they're so slow they'll get you killed" group. As you may guess, the truth is somewhere in between.

There are a lot of misconceptions about point shooting and its viability, due to different definitions of what point fire is, different ways to perform it, and different views held by some regarding the value of sighted fire. As far as methodology goes, we have shooting from "retention," with the gun barely out of its holster and the target at arms-length distance. Then there's shooting one-handed from the hip in a manner similar to the old FBI crouch, with the elbow just in front of the hip. Others shoot from a more or less upright position, with the pistol partly or fully extended in front of the center of the torso, but at abdomen or chest level and with either one or two hands. Let's take a look at separating some of the facts from the myths:

1) One can sooner learn to shoot with consistent accuracy at any distance, even up close, via sighted fire, rather than point fire.
2) One can sooner learn quick, if not necessarily fast, consistent accuracy at any distance via sighted fire than they can quick and accurate point fire between distances of four and 12 yards.

3) Shooters can sooner learn much better all-around shooting habits through sighted fire than point.

4) Those who advocate training methods and performance styles that conform to the body's instinctive/reflexive responses to danger to the exclusion of all else (which encompasses some point-shooting training) have a good point, when minimal training will be given to people with no prior experience and who will probably not engage in rigorous continued training. For such shooting students, this is probably the fastest way to program in some minimal amount of technique that might stick. However, when such training consists of only point shooting, I do not believe it allows for a very high level of performance across all the potential skill sets a shooter should have. It is worth noting that hard training will supplant instinctive (genetic) reactions with programmed reflexive reactions, so it's worthwhile researching which techniques allow the highest potential performance, as opposed to ease of learning.

5) Those who say you won't have time in a real fight to take a "correct" position, aim properly with sights, or perform a careful trigger squeeze and, so, you must learn some speedy and "instinctive" form of style, are both right and wrong. It is true you probably won't have time to waste in a dire, personal-defense situation (though you should remember your Condition Yellow/Orange mindset will help buy you time in the way of being prepared both mentally and as physically as possible for a situation to go south). It's also true that, if you don't properly train yourself, you will perform too slowly, just as it's true that, if you do properly train, you can perform almost every shooting technique in this book at about the same speed as any point-shooting technique I'm currently aware of, but with visually verifiable accuracy. A properly trained shooter can take a "correct," non-instinctive position just as fast as an instinctive one. Their subconscious trigger reflex, done without disturbing the gun, is just as fast as a trigger yank that disturbs the gun, and you already know how fast a flash sight picture can be seen. The question is, how willing are you to put in the work to gain such skills? The one practical speed exception to point shooting I'll grant is

the time difference needed between getting a gun aligned on the target at hip level versus eye level (though that also includes some serious accuracy differences).

6) Accurate and fast sighted fire requires the shooter learn and possess those necessary skill sets. Many of those skills are missing from point-fire methods—and if point shooting is all student studies, he misses out completely.

7) Point fire is a necessary skill, but one that should follow learning the sighted fire skill sets, so the shooter can apply them as necessary/appropriate to a point-fired shot.

8) Competence with a pistol requires knowing both techniques thoroughly and being able to reflexively, subconsciously, and successfully apply whichever is appropriate to solve the immediate problem. This may even include switching back and forth—instantly—as targets appear at different distances. In that vein alone, the whole always-this versus never-that argument is moot.

Given my innate preference for sighted-fire skills, as well as my recognition that point fire skills are also necessary, how do you morph sighted skills into point skills in the most seamless and easy way possible? Let's start at distances where you would use sighted fire (a skill set you should now be comfortable with), but on which you could still actually get your hits in slightly faster time without it through slight changes in technique.

At distances of, say, six to 10 yards and using your normal presentation to eyesight level, you can often get away with looking "through" the sights, i.e., looking along the line of the sights but focusing on the target. You would be aware of the blurry gun being centered in the target. In such circumstances, it is possible to hit well, primarily due to your good physical hand alignment, the size and proximity of the target, and the fact that you can still see where your gun is pointing, if not precisely aiming.

Another way to describe this type of shooting is what I think of as "index shooting." With sufficient training time in sighted fire, your two hands will reflexively bring the gun into a near-perfect alignment index on almost any size or distanced target via your brain having used the sights as a visual guide to teach your hands what to do. This ingrained reflexive alignment should be good enough, on a large close target, to hit the desired area without having to check your aim via sight picture focus.

It is a form of point shooting done not from the hip, but from the eye level. It requires and uses the ingrained muscle memory of a very large number of practice gun presentations to develop. Its benefit is that it allows the highest possible combination of speed and certainty of hits at close range, due to the gun being positioned along or near your sight line (which allows some peripheral vision feedback). Caution: too much of

Performance Standards

The Bill Drill is a fairly well-recognized practice regime that has performance standards, i.e., times in which the drill should be performed. The suggested performance standards for the Bill Drill and other techniques discussed in this chapter are as follows:

1) Draw and fire two reasonable center hits (no more than six inches apart) at seven yards in 1.5 seconds, from concealment.

2) Fire both controlled and dedicated pair splits with good recognized sight pictures at a seven-yard target. You should perform this drill with times between shots and fair center hits in less than $3/10$-second split times.

3) Be able to correct a bad second sight picture of a split to get a good hit and still get a split time of around 3/10-second or less.

4) Fire accurate hammers and index-point pairs at two- to five-yard targets with good hits in under $2/10$-second between shots.

5) Run a Bill Drill from the holster, with all center hits, in under four seconds.

Completing these drills successfully will put you in a very high percentile of overall handgun competence performance, probably over the ninety-fifth percentile of handgun owners and a little under, or close to, mid-level in practical shooting competition. This is the mental and physical skill set you must strive to achieve to hit one single target with consistent accuracy and life-saving speed. Anything less and you are kidding yourself.

How much intense, correct, regular practice is your life worth? Are you willing to dry-fire one to three hours a week, every week? How about live-fire 200-plus rounds in a practice session at least twice a month? Between the possibilities of failing to effectively defend yourself and hitting an innocent bystander with a missed shot, you probably should not be carrying a gun if you are not willing to put in the work to reach a level of shooting that does not result in either of those two endings. Your gun's mere presence may not save you. Your mindset and skill are what count. Think carefully ... and train hard.

shooting this way can carry this technique over to shots where you really *need* to see your sights, so be careful about when and where you use it. You must train often enough to be aware and in control of the technique you are performing.

Eventually, physical muscle memory skill can carry over to target alignment with the gun below your sight line, anywhere from a few inches below eye level and center chest just out from the ready position. At this point, your eyes will be locked on the target point you want to hit, the gun in your peripheral view only. You will not see your sights, only a blurry gun. Since you will not have a sight picture to activate your trigger finger, use the final position of the gun as the tactile, rather than your usual visual, cue to shoot. Once you master the look-through-the-sights technique at a given maximum distance, try it with your handgun at the level of your chin with your arms about three-quarters extended. Again, see what your maximum accuracy range is. Next, shoot with the gun at chest level and arms half extended. In other words, start at the known success datum (sighted fire), and move off that datum only at very short distance into the unknown (looking through the sights at eyesight level), and train to make that your next known skill datum. Then move a short distance into the next unknown, step by step, proceeding only after consistent success has been attained at the last step.

Understand that the motion of the presentation from the holster using a two-handed grip will be the same whether to eyesight line with full arm extension or mid-torso with half extension. The only difference will be in how high you raise the gun and how far you push out. The farther the target, the higher you raise and further extend the gun. At three to six yards, you should be have acceptable hits with a half-extended gun held mid-torso to chest level (well below eyesight line).

ONE-HANDED SHOOTING

To proficiently shoot one-handed and unsighted, the gun presented just a bit forward from and above the hip, I suggest you first work your way slowly and steadily with two hands from the eyesight level down to a position in front of your navel with your upper arms being in full contact against your ribs. If you can hit from there out to three to five yards, next try the draw and presentation to the same position without bringing your support hand into the grip, but continuing to position the gun arm as you did when using both hands.

This last presents the problem of keeping your support hand indexed someplace, so it doesn't wander in front of the muzzle. I like to keep my support forearm against my center chest with palm and fingers flat on my chest. That effectively keeps me from shooting off my own fingers.

WHAT ABOUT LASERS?

A laser on your handgun will show you where the thing is aimed without shooting expensive ammo to put holes in targets. I don't personally like using a laser; I find it takes longer to find the dot on the target than get a good presentation and flash sight picture. Still, I'll acknowledge that, for point shooting practice, it might pay for itself in unexpended ammo.

TARGETS

Up till now, you will have been shooting at whatever target type you have selected. I suggest that, if you have not selected a humanoid target of some type, you should do so. Practice on primarily making hits to the upper center chest area, but also work on head shots in the area of the eye sockets. Another target area for consideration is the pelvis/hip area. If your local criminals start wearing body armor, you will have to shoot them above or below the armor.

TACTICS OR BASICS?

I have not wanted to delve into the "tactical" aspects of fighting in this book, preferring, instead, to focus on pure marksmanship. This is the building block that comes before anything else, and it is what I see most missing when I observe others. Too, there are few good resources of relevant information available. Sure, there are plenty of tactical references out there regarding how to behave in a fight, and I commend you to study them. But if you're looking for a reference on the most important building blocks of solid shooting skills, I believe this is the book that will get you there.

If you are a beginner, you will have to perform at the conscious level first, allowing time and repetition to provide a path to the subconscious process. Just keep working on those controlled pairs in order to maintain accuracy and drill in the automatic physical and mental reflexes and perceptions.

CHAPTER 10

MULTIPLE TARGET TRANSITIONS

There are two basic ways of transitioning from target to target. One is to "look" your sights onto the next target. This means keeping your eye focused on your sights as you swing the gun onto the next target, making sure you maintain correct alignment between front and rear sights as you move the gun. The target will be blurry as it slides behind the sights. In the second method, you'll take your eye off your sights, search out the next target, bring the gun across to it, and re-acquire your sight focus as the gun covers the new target.

Two close targets, two far targets. Vary the order in which you engage them.

I find I use both methods, but under different circumstances. In situations where I know I have a "shoot" target (that is, it's a known that there's no decision to be made about whether or not the target is to be shot), I "look" my sights over to targets that are within about 30 or so degrees of arc apart. This is a very fast method, because you keep the shooting focus on your front sight and you already know what your sight picture looks like as it arrives on the new target. For any range of motion beyond that 30-degree limitation, or where an unknown situation is presenting itself (and a target might need to be first identified as being one that needs to be shot), I use the eye-search method. In either event, three things are necessary to hit the new target: getting the gun to the new target, seeing your sight picture, and controlling the movement of the gun.

In moving the gun sideways, you should pivot from the waist, knees, and ankles; try to keep the relationship of your extended

Looking to the next target while the prior shot's empty case is still on its way up.

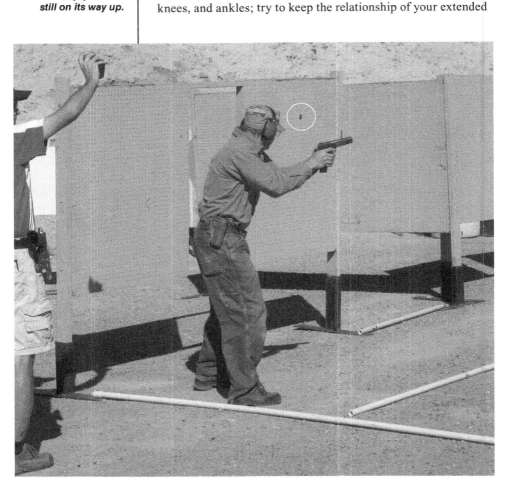

arms and upper body the same as when standing still. Think of your upper body as a gun turret on a tank or battleship. Your upper body from the waist up is your gun mount. Keep it intact whenever possible; avoid pushing just your hands and arms sideways. Know that if the angle of pivot gets past about 45 degrees, some pivoting of the feet may become necessary and, if much more pivot is required, it may be necessary to step around with your feet.

Much the same as in presenting the gun from the holstered or ready position, your focus may have to transition from the target to the sights. Forgetting to do this usually results in a poor shot. The gun should be brought to a stop dead in the middle of the target after your eyes find the sights. This will prevent you from over-swinging and shooting past your desired impact point.

Shooting with a moving gun is possible, but tricky in that the time lag from the mental shoot command to the point where the

The plate rack. Plates fall backwards and out of sight when hit.

bullet leaves the muzzle will place your shot further out in your swinging motion than you would believe. Think of it like the clay bird shotgunner's mantra, in that you'll be "shooting where the target's going to be," except you're shooting at a stationary target, not one that's moving.

> In shooting with a moving gun, you have to develop a feel for shooting on the way in from the target edge to the target center.

For you to effect a correct hit while shooting with a moving gun, you have to develop a feel for shooting on the way in from target edge to center, firing just as the near edge of the center zone is reached and as the gun continues to swing smoothly across the target. Obviously, with different sizes and distances of target and differing speeds of the swing, it becomes pretty difficult to judge the correct point of discharge for every situation. Yes, this method is faster than stopping the gun, but it's only worthwhile to employ if you can pull it off consistently. A helpful technique is to bring the gun quickly to nearly the edge of the target, then transfer your focus to the sights as you slow it down sharply just as it crosses the target edge, "looking" your sights across the near half of the target towards the center. In this manner, you initiate a quick movement that becomes a slow controlled movement just before the shot. Personally I consider stopping the gun to be the more reliable method of the two and the easier to learn.

Whatever technique you use, your eye must always wind up back on the front sight so you can verify your sight picture before firing. This is especially crucial when you are moving the gun. Seeing your sights before the shot and controlling the gun motion will keep your accuracy under control. Smoothness of motion is more important than speed of motion. This can be practiced by setting up three or four targets about seven or so yards away, and about one to five yards apart. Simply work from one side to the other and back, reload, and repeat. This drill also works fine in dry-fire.

An advanced trick that competition shooters use to accelerate their overall shooting speed is the use of a single shooting cadence across multiple targets. Their split times for two shots on the same target are the same as their transition times between targets. The practicing of this has the effect of slowing down the split shots, so as to gain slightly better accuracy, while speeding up the transition times between targets to recoup the time. Such top-of-the-game shooters can run through four or five targets in a row, and you can't tell which interval is a transition and which is a split.

A nice, simple practice drill that covers three basic skill sets is to set up two targets at different ranges (say five and 12 yards

Working on a two-target transition drill.

out) and about 30 or so degrees apart from each other. Start with the gun holstered (or, if you're not quite up to that, in the ready position), draw (or present) to one target with one shot, then pivot and transition to the second target for one shot. Stay facing the second target, re-holster (or return to the ready position), then repeat the drill starting with that target and transitioning the other way to the other target. Then repeat starting with this last target. Back and forth, right and left transitions. After a while, you can add a second shot per target. This will really work your most basic and important skill sets of getting the gun into action for the first shot, getting the follow-up second shot, and perfecting a good transition.

CHAPTER 11

SHOOTING MOVING TARGETS

"Keep the gun moving during and after the shot. The lead will vary depending on the target speed and distance, and this is something best learned by trial and error."

This is quite an interesting topic, one probably worthy of its own book. But I'm going to simplify it, for the sake of space, to what has worked for me.

There are three basic ways to hit a moving target. The first is to aim at a point in space ahead of the target with a motionless gun and depend upon timing to fire the shot so that the bullet and target wind up in the same place at the same time. The second method is to move the gun faster than the target, starting from behind the target and swinging through the target to get ahead of it. You would approach this method with the sights moving exactly along the path of the target and fire at some predetermined point ahead of the target while keeping the gun in motion. The last method is to move the gun along with the target at the same rate of speed, but aiming some distance ahead of it ("leading" it, in shotgunners' parlance), to allow for target motion during bullet transit time.

The first method is difficult and seems to be used probably the least of the three, so we might as well forget about it. The second method, the "swing-through," is the method I happen to like to use with a shotgun myself, but have never attempted it with a pistol. The third method, a constant or maintained lead, is what I like to use with a pistol. It requires a slower and less violent motion of the gun and, thus, allows for better control and vision of the sights.

With pistol targets at close range, there's not a lot of lead required, maybe a few inches at most, but it must be consistent in that you have to keep the gun moving at the same rate of speed as the target, while judging both your sight alignment and your lead amount. Much as in shotgunning, stopping the gun when shooting almost guarantees a miss behind the target, as stopping the gun allows the target to move ahead of where the bullet will end up. You have to press off the shot while the gun is in motion and, like a shotgunner (or golfer), follow through on your swing during the pressing and after the shot is on its way.

Moving targets are somewhat difficult to set up, but the effort is worth a try to learn the skill. In hunting, we would prefer our quarry stand still for the shot, and it is considered bad form among many serious rifle hunters to take a shot at running game, especially if it is much beyond 30 or 40 yards or so. (European hunting is much different, with many countries actually requiring the successful completion of a marksmanship test that includes scoring on a running game target.) However, in an interpersonal confrontation, anything is possible. An opponent heading sideways for cover is to be expected, rather than considered an exception—unless you can act to drop your attacker in their tracks (preferably while *you* are moving to cover!) and before they realize they just made a horrible miscalculation. Remember, you can't afford to lose.

So, what can we set up? Perhaps the easiest is some form of bobbing or swinging target that pivots back and forth on a stand, with a weight at the bottom of the pivoting portion to provide the momentum for the swing and also to bring it to an eventual halt. In IPSC/USPSA competition, such targets are common, often partially hidden behind hard cover or a no-shoot target to spice things up.

Another method is to set up something similar to an old-fashioned clothesline on a pulley. A friend tugging on a rope can pull a target along such a setup strung between two trees. Even simpler is a rope tied between two trees or other posts, with a target-holder board sliding directly along the rope via screw eyes in the board. A separate cord running from either end of the target board through a snap link hooked on the rope where it goes around the tree (on the tree side of the rope knot), allows the cord to run back toward the firing line so that the target can be pulled in either direction. This is what I recently built, and it works like a charm—as long as you have a friend pulling for you!

When tracking the target, the amount of lead will depend upon both the target speed and its distance. For a far (say, 15 yards or more) and quick target, keep your sights moving just ahead of the leading edge of the desired hit zone, with correct front-to-

rear sight alignment. For a close (say, seven yards or less) target moving at a moderate to fast walk, you can pretty well hold right on the desired impact area. Keep the gun moving during and after the shot. The exact amount of lead will vary with target speed and distance, and while it is possible to calculate this by comparing target speed, bullet speed, and target distance, it's not a bad idea to learn it by trial and error. Too, having your friend madly jerk the target back and forth erratically will really drive you nuts; you'll have a hard time looking at your sights, since your eyes will want to remain glued to that unpredictable target.

Move with a smooth and level upper body.

In any event, gun movement to address a moving target is similar to gun movement when performing a target-to-target transition. It must be a controlled motion, and you must verify a moving sight picture before shooting. Smoothness, control, and keen focus on your sights will get you the results you need.

SHOOTING WHILE YOU ARE MOVING

This is another tough skill that can be mastered with a bit of the right technique. The main thing is to realize that normal walking motion creates a bit of up-and-down bobbing in your gun hold, as well as a less than smooth linear motion. If we can smooth out our progress and greatly reduce our up-and-down motion while on the move, we can end up with a smooth, controlled body motion that is not that different from that used in a target transition or when following a moving target.

For the sake of simplicity, let's assume our target is motionless. The first thing we need to do is learn to control our own motion. Running and hitting is pretty difficult and requires considerable practice, even at close range. Walking and hitting is another story. Our movement, from the self-defense point of view, should be away from the threat and towards cover, if possible. If you are in law enforcement or conceive of a situation where you have to rescue your family from a gang of attackers, then forward to cover or even closing right to the threat is what is called for.

Getting off the "X"

The first rule of shooter movement is known as "getting off the X," the X being the spot on which you are standing when your hand starts moving toward your handgun to draw and fire it. The direction of movement is to one side or the other, that is, perpendicular to your line of sight to your opponent. *Get out of his line of fire!* One or two steps sideways while drawing and firing will help you get ahead of your opponent's action/reaction cycle. Remember that, in a self-defense incident, you will be reacting to your opponent's actions; you start out behind the curve. Your sudden movement off line will help reverse this situation and gain you the upper hand.

Practice this drill with an empty handgun first and read your sight picture movement to learn to control it, before trying live fire.

Shooting While Walking

We need to learn to walk quickly in such a fashion as to produce a smooth and level motion of our upper body. By keeping the knees more deeply flexed than usual and using greater

Reloading on the move. I ought to be watching for the next target, instead of looking at the gun, but I can't walk and chew gum at the same time.

motion of all the leg and hip joints, we can walk with a sort of rolling motion of the lower body. In this manner, the natural up-and-down motion of walking is absorbed in greater flexing of the leg joints, from hip to knee to ankle. The resulting walk is a bit funny looking, being slightly reminiscent of the film antics of Groucho Marx, but it goes a long way towards keeping the upper body and extended gun steady.

If you must move and shoot, keep your knees more flexed than normal, so as to absorb the natural up and down motions of walking.

In order to do this, you have to lower your body slightly by bending your knees and hips to deepen your stance. The point in this is to keep your legs from reaching a fully straight extension, as they tend to do while normally walking. Here the legs are always in some form of flex, which tends to absorb the up-and-down bobbing normal walking creates. This allows the torso to move along in a more level motion. By being careful with our pacing cadence, this style also allows our linear motion to be less jerky. The result is movement more like riding in a car than walking.

When walking forwards or backwards, you should be facing the target. But, when the target is off to the side of our line of motion, things get a little trickier. If the target is to your support-hand side, we can twist our body around quite a bit and still use the two-hand hold. If the target is to your strong-hand side, a full 90-degree twist makes it extremely difficult, if not impossible, to keep your support hand out ahead of the strong hand and, at this point, you will probably be forced to use only the strong hand for shooting.

Shooting at a target that's off to one side at a shallow angle and ahead of us as we move obliquely towards it is probably the easiest angle to work with. As we approach a pivot-to-target angle of 90 degrees, our apparent motion in relation to the target seems greater and presents us with a more difficult shot. So, it would be good to spend some extra time on this situation in practice and to consider that, if we ever have to shoot on the move for real, we should try to solve the problem with good solid hits before we wind up at the perpendicular. If we get past the perpendicular in our movement and the target still requires behavioral correction, it is best to pivot as we move past the perpendicular and walk backwards from it while delivering fire.

CHAPTER 12

ONE-HANDED SHOOTING

"The odds of the skills of one-handed shooting being required in the real world may not be high, but the consequences of not having them, should their necessity be realized, might be terminal."

S ooner or later, you will realize that, in the real world of unexpected events, you may find one of your hands to be busy with something too important to interrupt when the time comes to shoot. Or you may be wounded either beforehand, or even during a fight by hostile fire before you can solve the problem. For any of those reasons, it's a good idea to hone your skills with each of your hands separately. The odds of requiring this skill in the real world may not be high, but the consequences of being incapable of them may be terminal.

TRANSITIONING THE GUN VERSUS THE WEAK-HAND DRAW

You may have to transition the gun from the strong hand to the weak hand, or you may have to get the gun into action from holster or purse with the weak hand to begin with. In a transition, make absolutely certain that the hand receiving the gun keeps its trigger finger straight and outside the trigger guard as the new grip is achieved! This is especially important when the weak hand is the receiver, since you may not have drilled the straight trigger finger reflex into that hand yet. If the gun is a semi-auto pistol with a safety built for a right-hander (and you are right-handed), disengage the safety with the right (strong) hand before transitioning the gun to the left hand.

The weak-hand draw motion depends, of course, on the way you carry the gun. A crossdraw or shoulder holster will have the

Reach behind your back with your weak hand and get a secure firing grip on pistol butt. Make sure your trigger finger remains straight.

Draw the pistol and move it to your weak side, keeping the muzzle down and trigger finger straight.

The pistol is now ready in your weak-hand grip. As the muzzle becomes pointed towards the target, disengage the safety with you trigger finger (if applicable).

Reach across with your weak hand, get a reversed grip on the pistol butt, and draw the pistol.

Rotate your hand and pistol 180 degrees and re-holster so that the butt points forward. Now, re-grip pistol with weak hand in a normal firing grip and draw.

gun on the same side of your body as the weak hand. This simplifies matters a bit, but you will still need a pretty good amount of wrist flexibility to withdraw the gun effectively. Such a setup, though, presents a safety issue. As the gun clears the holster and your wrist starts to straighten out, you will sweep the muzzle across your own body if you are not very careful about your movement.

If you are wearing a strong-side hip holster, you'll have a bit of an awkward reach drawing with your weak hand. The best way to start this kind of draw is to crouch a bit, stick out your fanny, and lean your upper body forwards. This allows some separation between the gun butt and the side of your body, which permits the weak hand to sneak in there behind your back and get a grip. Don't forget to train your weak hand trigger finger to stay straight outside the trigger guard! You must also remember to move the gun straight up out of the holster, though the inclination may be to drag it out sideways. Once you've grasped the gun securely, bring it across your back while keeping the muzzle pointed down and away from your backside. Get a proper firing grip on it as you bring it around to the weak side, so you can present it immediately if necessary.

Weak hand-only and strong-hand-only practice should be an essential part of your practice routine.

Again, Kelly McCann's superb *Crucible* series shows an excellent sequence of this.

If your holster is at such a position and angle that you can't reach it from behind with your weak hand, go around from the front. Grab the gun butt in a natural motion with the palm facing in towards your body (your grip will look upside-down on the gun butt), lift the gun up from the holster, twist your wrist palm-outwards to reverse the gun butt direction from rearwards to forwards, then re-holster it as far as it will go. It will now be positioned butt forward (the gun backwards in the holster), and you

Shooting a strong hand-only requirement at an IPSC match.

can re-grip and re-draw the gun in a natural cross-draw fashion with the weak hand.

SHOOTING ONE-HANDED

When it comes to firing, you should have few problems with the strong hand only, though you will note that your hold is somewhat less steady and much less resistant to recoil. With the weak hand, however, you will probably find that you have precious little trigger control. You will have to train the weak trigger finger from scratch to perform properly. This can easily be done with dry fire, so be committed to put in some time on it. Your body posture should be the same as for your two-handed grip, to keep things simple, and having the gun-side foot forward a bit, with your body turned away from the gun side in the old target-shooter stance does tend to be a bit more comfortable.

CHAPTER 13

PRACTICE DRILLS

L et's first describe drills that practice your individual skills. In this fashion you can test them and evaluate them one at a time and, thus, have a way to cure any deficiencies realized. After that, we'll look at drills that test these skills in practical combinations.

Train, train, and train some more. Stay focused.

SAFETY

Remember the four safety rules. What? Forgot them already? Go back to the end of the introduction and re-read, please! You will be required to obey all four when running these drills. Remember to keep the muzzle in a safe direction and not let it swing sideways toward any other shooter, re-member to keep your finger off the trigger until the sights are on the target, and obey whatever other range rules exist.

MINDSET

Make up a list of specific exercises for each session, including the results you desire. Clear your mind of any extraneous, irrelevant thoughts before starting, and think through the movements of the drill step by step. Perform the whole drill in your mind first, then perform it in dry-fire, before switching to live-fire. Stay focused, call your shots, remember your sight pictures, and compare them to the target results. Record your results on a notepad. Include all issues, along with any solutions or breakthroughs you have.

TARGETS

You may start with something like a large bull's-eye or simple paper dinner plate, but at some point you'll want to switch to a humanoid target; ones with faces and a gun point-ing at you are good to train yourself to recognize a threat. Remember Chapter One's subject, mindset? Remember the visual cue "mental trigger" that sends you from Condition Orange to Condition Red? Another thing you can do (if your range facility allows) is to mix several non-hostile targets with one or two threatening targets. This helps your mind prepare for the reality of recognition and decision making.

TIMER

To make the most of your sessions, you should seriously consider investing in a shot timer. It will give accurate read-ings to $1/100$-second of your progress and let you know where you need to spend extra training energy.

TAPE

A roll of masking tape will be useful for covering holes in the target and prolonging your target life. You don't necessar-ily have to tape your holes on each run of a drill, but do make a note of the results of each run. If you switch from one drill to another, first study the hole patterns from the drill you just shot. This is your learning moment. Then, tape all the holes and move on to the next drill. Each drill will have its own form of error potential, so you'll want to be able to isolate the results to learn what you are doing right and wrong for each drill.

THE PROCESS

You are performing a specific process when you fire a shot. See and be aware of the process—flash sight picture, surprise break, and recoil recovery—and be in control of the process. With every shot, make a call, see the front sight lift in recoil, and see the sights realign after recoil recovery. This is the only way you will advance. Any other way and you will be wasting time and ammo.

THE SIMPLEST DRILL: THE PRESENTATION FROM READY

This is an excellent drill for your basic skill of guiding the handgun to the target to achieve a proper sight picture. It is especially good for dry-firing at home. The more reps you can

In the ready position, trigger finger straight, safety on if applicable, eyes on target. Raise up the gun to sight line and focus on the front sight before extending the gun forward. This is the quickest way to see your sights. The safety, if there is one, comes off as the gun comes up.

perform, the faster you will train your hands. Set your target at about seven yards to start. Here's the drill:

1. Start at the ready position, forearms retracted to your chest and gun muzzle depressed, safety on if applicable, trigger finger straight, grip (remember the thumb lines) and stance (staggered feet, knees bent, fanny low, and forward lean) correct, eyes on the target right on the spot you want your bullet to go.
2. Raise the gun to your sight line, so it appears between your eyes and the target.
3. Shift your visual focus to your front sight.
4. Press out the handgun to full extension while focusing on (and evaluating) your sight picture—proper sight alignment against the target, maintaining intense front sight focus — keeping the forward body lean and pushing your shoulders toward the target.

Extending forward, while focusing on the front sight and evaluating the sight picture. Once you see your sights, your finger can touch the trigger. Fully extended forward. If your sight picture is correct when your hands stop moving, fire.

5. When the gun stops at full extension, do a flash sight picture check, correct if necessary, and then press the trigger without disturbing the sight alignment. Make just one shot to start with, but follow through by seeing the entire recoil cycle of the front sight lift, calling your shot, seeing the sights recover back down, and judging the new sight picture. Do this visual follow-through on every shot. It is the only way you will be able to shoot successive shots quickly and accurately.

Start with these steps distinctly and individually at first, but realize your goal is to blend them into one smooth motion that results in a correct sight picture, achieved by the hands, as the gun stops its forward movement, so that you can fire at the moment it stops and without a pause between stopping and firing. This is the simplest drill you can do and one of best. Once you become smooth and accurate in this drill, you can modify it slightly so that your target is at 10 or 15 yards or further, or

Start the draw. Grip and grab, trigger finger straight, trigger-hand thumb flagged in hitchhiker position. This is also where your hands should be when you re-holster. Clear the holster. The trigger finger is still straight, the safety is still on.

so that you are shooting before full extension at a target closer than seven yards.

Once you get proficient at this, progress to firing two shots, with full follow-through after each shot. Don't consciously stop the process after the second trigger squeeze because you only intended to shoot two; in the real world, you won't always control when you are done—the target(s) will have a say in that. Stay in the game in case you need one more un-expected shot. Or another! Follow through completely to the post-recoil flash sight picture, even when you know it's your last shot. Call every shot and know if you threw a bad one without having to see the hole in the target. This is so impor-tant. Stay focused on your sights and see everything your gun is showing you.

Your first concern is accuracy. Time is of the essence in every drill, but accuracy comes first. You should be keeping your shots in a six-inch group. If that sounds large, remember that you have a lot of target area that all counts the same, so

Rotate the gun's muzzle downrange, then the gun comes to the support hand, which forms the proper grip position and pressure. When the muzzle points downrange, disengage the safety (if applicable). Raise up the gun to sight line and acquire the front sight, as in the presentation drill.

use it. (You really have more than six inches, but try to maintain that tightness so you don't let speed make you too sloppy.)

A good presentation should give you the required accuracy in well under one second. If you have a shot timer, you can work to shave it down to a half-second.

THE DRAW

You will be holstering a "hot" (fully loaded gun) for these drills. Remember to keep your finger off the trigger, and don't grab the holster with your support hand when you holster, or you'll sweep the muzzle across your hand. Learn to safely holster with one hand, trigger finger straight, without pointing the gun at your leg or hip, and without looking at your holster. You can do this at home with an empty gun in dry-fire—work on it!

As described earlier, the draw is your bread-and-butter drill. If it feels clumsy at first, you can break it down into pieces. Start with your hands doing the grip-and-grab: both hands move together, the firing hand to the full firing grip on the handgun with a straight trigger finger outside the holster, the support hand correctly positioned under the strong-side pectoral muscle. Check that your hands are correct. If they are, draw and clear the holster, rotate the muzzle downrange, click off the safety, and join hands. Stop and check your joining of hands and proper grip (thumb lines) before moving the gun forwards. Then finish the presentation as in the prior drill.

One shot should do at first, including the follow-through of seeing the sight lift in recoil and then recover. When those single shots are going where you want them to in a smooth fluid motion, add a second shot as quickly as you can control the recoil and see the sight picture recover, making sure to follow through on the second shot. Remember, stay in control of your movements. Go slowly at first. Slow makes for correct and smooth, and smooth makes fast.

Your goal, as in the first drill, is to create one smooth motion resulting in a flash sight picture and an accurate shot fired as the gun stops moving forward. A center hit in less than 1.5 seconds from concealed leather is fair, and two center hits in that time is better.

TRANSITIONS

Set up two targets, about one yard apart from each other and five yards away from you. Draw or present from ready to one target, fire two rounds, then transition to the other target for two more shots. Work right to left, left to right, until you are smooth and comfortable with it.

A well-executed draw-and-shoot-two drill.

Increase the distance both between the two and away from you until you are working about 12 to 15 yards distance from you to the targets and six to 10 yards between the targets. Then, push one of these targets two or three times further away. This adds a change in your accuracy requirement, which will also change the cadence of your shooting from the close target to the far target. Draw to and shoot one round in the closer target as fast as you can get a good hit, then transition to the far one as fast as you can get a good hit (which should take a bit more time). Reverse the engagement order and try going slower to faster. This will help teach you to switch speed gears while maintaining the required accuracy.

Next, bring the two targets back to about seven yards out and place them one yard apart. Now add a third and fourth tar-

The El Presidente starting position.

get, much further to either side of the first two, creating a larger transition angle. One should be close (three to four yards), one far (12 to 15 yards). They should require at least a 45-degree transition from the two targets in the center. Pivot your body with and without moving your feet. Draw to the two targets in front of you and engage them, then make the big swing to one side to a third target. Make a big swing right, then do the drill over, center to left. Then perform it center to one side, swing-

1) Turn first and then draw.

2) Clearing the holster.

3) The speed reload. The old magazine is falling past the target stand base. I ought to have my eyes on target.

4) Engaging the left target.

ing all the way over to the opposite side target, to complete an eight-shot drill. (If your handgun doesn't hold that many, use one shot per target instead of two). Work this drill in both directions.

For the targets set seven yards away and one yard apart, a ½-second between hits is fair, ⅓-second is better. Anything else is dependant upon how far apart and how far away.

Here is where you will find some of your shots spread left or right on the target, due to over or under swinging the gun to the target. Work to see your sights stop in the middle of the target before firing.

RELOADS

Using the transition drill above, shoot one or two rounds at each target, perform a speed reload, then re-shoot with your transition movement in the opposite direction. You might want to bring a carpet scrap to lay in front of you, in order to keep your magazines or speedloaders from hitting a concrete surface or landing in dirt or sand. With a semi-auto, practice speed reloads both shooting to slide lock on an empty gun and reloading with a round still in the chamber. In both, you should let the magazine in the gun fall free. Also, practice the tactical save-magazine load, where you swap a full magazine for a partial, pocketing the partially empty magazine. This is a good thing to do before re-holstering in preparation for the next

5) Transitioning to the center target.

6) Seating the new magazine.

drill. With a wheelgun, practice with both loose rounds and speedloaders. Let the empty cases hit the ground.

THE "EL PRESIDENTE"

This timed drill is a good skill yardstick. Three humanoid targets are set 10 yards away, a yard apart from each other, and the three in an even line. You'll begin by facing up range (away from the targets). In the official competition version, you stand in a square of angle iron or PVC pipe, with your toes touching the rear-most border and your hands up in "surrender" position. On the start signal, you turn and then draw—not the reverse! *Never* draw first and then turn! Engage each target with two shots, perform a speed reload, then shoot them twice each again. All center hits ("A"-zone on a USPSA target) in 10 seconds or less was what Col. Cooper considered a par score for competence. Top-end competitors can do it in about half the time, some even less. (Full disclosure: my best was about seven-point-something seconds while dropping one point with a hit outside an "A"-zone.)

MOVEMENT

Warning! Do not try this drill until you are comfortable with safe, stationary shooting! This is "getting off the X," or getting out of your opponent's line of aim as you are drawing and firing. You'll disrupt his flow of action this way.

Go back and study the chapter on shooting while moving. Step sideways to either side as you draw and fire. Step diagonally to the side and rear combined, as well. Remember, your goal is to get away from the line along which your opponent will be aiming at you—movement straight to the rear doesn't do this.

Start with one target. Practice one step/one shot, then multiple steps/multiple shots, then multiples on multiple targets as you're moving. Make sure there is nothing to trip over in the direction you are moving! If you do trip over your own feet, get your finger off the trigger as soon as you realize your balance is lost, and keep the muzzle in a safe direction!

If your range facility allows, set up some form of object behind which to hide. This is called "cover" or "concealment" and sometimes a "barricade," on a practice range. Be very clear about their definitions. Cover, also called "hard cover," not only hides you, it would stop whatever type of bullet (handgun, rifle, etc.) is being shot at you. Concealment hides you, but is not bulletproof. If your opponent knows you are there, he can still shoot through concealment to hit you (and vice-versa, so use this wisely). Also remember that, while one object may stop handgun bullets or shotgun buckshot, it may be merely concealment to more powerful rifle bullets. For practice, something as simple as a sheet of box cardboard on a target stand is all that's necessary. Only one is needed.

Practice moving from the open to cover as you draw and shoot. Set cover in any direction that has an open line of fire between you and your target(s), as you start the drill standing on the imaginary "X." At the start of the drill, move (move!) off the "X" while drawing and firing your first (or more) shots. Get behind cover and practice continuing to engage the target(s) from either side of cover. Only expose your handgun, hands, and your eyes to the target. Practice in all directions in which you can do so safely.

Plate racks are a great drill to work on, if available.

MALFUNCTION CLEARANCE DRILLS

These will be as detailed in Chapter Eight. Set yourself up for each one as described below. I would suggest first buying some snap-caps (plastic dummy cartridges) or, if you reload, make up dummy rounds. Try these drills first with dummy rounds before trying with live ammunition, and get familiar with the movements before trying for speed. Also, watch out for any sharp edges on your handgun, as they can make you bleed while doing these drills full speed. Serious handgunners will get such things rounded off and smoothed by a gunsmith.

A .22 rimfire is a great practice gun, cheap to shoot and almost without recoil. The girl is taking the old classic Weaver stance.

For the following drills, once you have fixed the problem, re-acquire your two-handed grip and pause to perform a visual/mental assessment of the situation. On the range, obviously you can keep shooting, but, in real life, your target may have disappeared or fallen to your previous shots, or some innocent bystander might be running through your line of aim (in front of or behind your target), as you bring the gun back into aiming position. Train yourself to see what is in front of you and decide what to do.

You can vary the drills to continue shooting a still-active threat or assess that the threat is over, then perform a tactical save-magazine change and re-holster. Remember, a malfunction will interrupt your processes of seeing, deciding, and acting. You must get back on track with the situation in front of you after you fix the malfunction. A mistake here may cause you to kill or injure an innocent person. Train accordingly!

The results of four draw-and-shoot-two drills. Note the high shot, which was the second shot of the last drill. The timer tells the reason why in the next photo.

Tap-Rack-Ready

The slide is forward on an empty chamber, hammer/striker is cocked, but the loaded magazine not quite latched in place. Aim, press trigger, get a click instead of a bang, tap the magazine hard, rack the slide, assess to continue shooting or not.

Stovepipe

As you carefully ease the slide closed, chambering a live round, insert an empty case vertically in the ejection port so that its base (the primer end) holds the slide slightly open. Aim, see the case blocking your sight picture, wipe it away with the support hand, reestablish your grip, assess to continue shooting or not.

Double Feed

Starting with a completely empty pistol, lock back the slide, place an empty case in the chamber, then insert a loaded magazine. Drop the slide forward, which will ram the nose of the top magazine cartridge up against the base of the empty case in the chamber and create the double feed. Aim, press, nothing happens. Look, lock back the slide, strip the magazine, cycle the slide till the chamber is empty, reload your magazine (preferably a new one), rack the slide and let it slam shut to chamber a round, re-grip, assess. Try for a four-second clearance.

Revolver Malfunctions

For revolvers, practice firing two or three rounds, opening the cylinder, extracting one or two rounds or empties, and reloading with one or two loose rounds from belt loops or pocket, before assessing to continue or not. That will give you a real dexterity workout. Doing it by feel in the pitch-dark without a hiccup is the skill you want to achieve.

My overall time for the last drill on that target was 1.49 seconds. The time between first and second shots (the split time) was 0.16-second. I shot the second shot too fast, before the gun fully recovered from recoil, which is why it was high out of the group (see previous page).

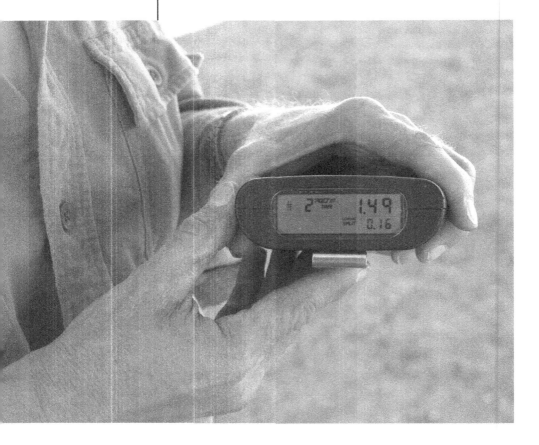

Real Malfunctions

If your handgun happens to "malf" unexpectedly, all by itself, while running a shooting drill, don't stop and stare at it in surprise while turning it sideways. Fix it! You will never have a better opportunity to fix a problem than when it is actually happening on the practice range. Fix it, keeping the muzzle downrange, then assess to continue. This is exactly the response you'll need in real life, right? Make the most of such opportunities. Learn not to be surprised into inaction!

> *Have a malfunction during a practice session? Don't dawdle with it! Move with haste to fix the problem, just as you would in a real-world fight for your life.*

LEARNING

Each time you shoot a drill, you must study the results. Each hole will teach you something.

First, make sure you call each shot you fire. When looking at the target, the holes should match your calls. If you have wild shots you didn't call, this tells you you're blinking and flinching. If you remember calling a bad one in your sight picture, it should be reflected on the target. If you called them all good and they went where you called them, then you are doing things right. If you called some questionable shots due to imperfect sight picture, this is where you start learning about your *acceptable* sight picture. Make note of where the imperfect shots went. If they hit well enough, you file that sight picture away in your memory, along with the bullet hole position and distance to the target. This is how you can trade a little accuracy for a little speed, while still knowing what the result will be before you fire the shot.

CHAPTER 14

PROFESSIONAL TRAINING AND COMPETITION

Paul firing his .40 S&W Limited Class pistol in a USPSA/IPSC match. The fellow behind him with his hand out is the Range Officer, holding a shot timer.

PROFESSIONAL TRAINING

There are a number of established shooting schools that offer intense and comprehensive training in the practical use of rifles, shotguns, and pistols for various applications. These classes range from two or three days to five days. The Gunsite Training Academy in Prescott, Arizona, founded by the late Col. Jeff Cooper, in 1976 (it was first called the American Pistol Institute), is probably

the oldest and the one that set the standard for all that followed. Thunder Ranch (formerly in Texas, now in Oregon), run by Clint Smith (a former operations manager for Gunsite) employs a similar curriculum and is widely considered to be the best shooting school in the world. Both schools run a wide variety of classes from general to highly specialized and with all sorts of firearms. There are other schools as well, such as Tom Russell's American

Bonnie firing her .38 Super Unlimited (also known as "Open") Class pistol with its red dot optical sight and muzzle brake. Ladies do very well in this sport.

Another young lady works her way through a stage.

Firearms Academy, Chuck Taylor's American Small Arms Academy, Jim McKee's Shootrite Academy, Ron Avery's Practical Shooting Academy, and Dr. Ignatius Piazza's Front Sight Institute.

From the handgun perspective, the General Pistol 250 at Gunsite and Defensive Handgun 1 at Thunder Ranch roughly correspond to the material in this book. Investigation of these schools' websites will show what is currently offered. There are also a

number of individual trainers who will come to your location. It pays to do some research to find out who is good—and this is where hanging around competition shooters can come in handy.

My own experience with professional schools is limited to one General Rifle and one General Pistol class run by Col. Cooper. They were well worth every cent, in particular the pistol class, where I learned more in five and a half days than I had learned in

Reloading on the move, heading for the next target group ...

... which is through the door. Notice she does not allow the muzzle to point at her right arm.

literally 20 years of puttering around on my own! Between the material taught and the watchful eyes of good instructors, the students come out far ahead of where they were when they went in. The pacing of the classes can be quite intense at times, though the instructors are always helping you along.

In no way can you learn more in less time—as long as you pick the right school or instructor—and the difference between an untutored student on the first morning and the graduate will

be an order of magnitude. If you can spare the time and money, such a school will be one of the best skill investments you can possibly make.

COMPETITION

Next to professional training, the best thing to get you learning faster and learning better is engaging in some form of competition. Here you will get to mix with some very accomplished shooters,

Leaning out for a difficult shot. The white target represents a no-shoot target (i.e., a hostage, perhaps), and the shooter has to miss that while hitting the tan cardboard target behind it.

most of whom are usually quite willing to share their expertise with newcomers. You also get to shoot while a whole bunch of people are watching! While that concept can be quite forbidding to some, and some forms of competition require highly specialized and expensive equipment (either to be competitive or to conform to the rules), you should undertake every effort to find out just what sorts of competitions are held in your area. Not all have stringent requirements. Even showing up to watch and talk to some of the shooters allows you to learn quite a bit.

The formal types of competition are quite well established. Let's start with bull's-eye target shooting. NRA pistol bull's-eye is done with both .22 rimfire and centerfire handguns at ranges out to 50 yards. It consists of slow fire and timed rapid fire from the standing position, using one hand.

These matches are edifying to watch. They can also be intimidating. Don't let this put you off, however. Have a talk with the shooters and the match crew and find out what it takes to at least give it a try. Often you will find someone happy to not only coach you, but loan you a spare handgun for the match! Some clubs even have regular clinics for new shooters that allow them test the waters with borrowed equipment and good coaching.

Such a clinic is a purely golden opportunity to try something new and rub shoulders with people who are expert at the game—and they'll be coaching you.

Metallic silhouette shooting uses steel plate animal cut-outs for targets. This kind of competition originated for rifles at distances out to 500 meters, but there is a centerfire pistol version, too.

Clubs affiliated with the U.S. Practical Shooting Association (USPSA) hold what are known as practical handgun matches. These are events geared more towards fast action, close range, multiple target setups that encourages high-speed, high round-count shooting. Again, simply showing up to watch is a risk-free and logical first step. The competition pictures here are all from a local USPSA practical match. Look on www.uspsa.org to find your local club.

An even better place to start is the International Defensive Pistol Association (IDPA). Its matches are lower key than the run-and-gun USPSA matches, and IDPA's emphasize proper tactics (use of cover, not exposing yourself to your opponent, etc.), and accuracy over sheer speed. They are a bit easier for new shooters to try out, and they will help start the formation of good habits. Look on www.idpa.com.

Left: Holstering and almost ready for "Shooter ready? Stand by," followed by the timer beep ... .

Right: ... and away we go!

Around the barricade. Feet have to stay inside the rectangle.

Beyond this, there are many clubs that will have informal matches of an endless variety. There is no limit to the imagination of people looking to have fun and some friendly competition. These are all chances to test your mettle, evaluate your hard-won skills under some varying degrees of pressure, make new friends, and learn quite a bit in a friendly atmosphere. Don't be shy, get out and test the waters!

Broken bones don't stop left-handed Steve from shooting the match one-handed — and from his weak side! Well, maybe Steve doesn't have a weak side.

NEW!

HANDGUN TRAINING
FOR PERSONAL PROTECTION

Richard A. Mann

How To Choose & Use The Best Sights, Lights, Lasers & Ammunition

This is an excerpt from the new Gun Digest book
*Handgun Training for Personal Protection,
by Richard A. Mann.*

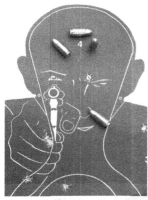

The Laser's Edge

"The world is full of obvious things which nobody by any chance ever observes."
—*Sherlock Holmes,* The Hound Of Baskervilles

E arly on, I think most everyone, including me, thought of lasers as a replacement for sights. That concept of the laser sight was what I resisted. Now that I have experience with them, at work and at play, I can admit I may have initially overlooked the obvious. They are *not* a replacement for sights. In short, I was wrong.

When I decided to get serious about lasers, my first impulse was to find out if I could shoot as accurately with a laser as I could with open sights. I conducted several drills, some timed and others at my own pace, from as close as 10 yards and as far away as 50. I found there was no discernible difference in group size between the two sight systems on what was, at that time, my issue Glock Model 23. However, I was able to shoot tighter groups with a Crimson Trace Laser Grip-equipped snubnose revolver.

I also discovered that, if you want to shoot from the hip, the laser offered the shooter who is unpracticed in this art a much higher level of speed and accuracy. And, at the risk of stating the obvious, I will add that, in the dark or low light, the laser performed better than tritium night sights.

As I looked for other tangible, on-target ways to compare sights and lasers I realized, like Holmes said, I was overlooking the obvious. It's not a sights versus lasers question. So I'll leave the description of my shoot-out, if you want to call it that, confined to the above summary. What really needed investigation was if a laser offered any benefit to the shooter and what, if any, were its detractors. In short, do they work, how can they be used to the shooter's advantage, and are they worth the money?

My first important discovery was that the laser was a tremendous aid to dry-fire practice. Picking a spot on the wall or target with an (for damn sure) unloaded gun, it was an enlightening experience to watch the little red dot wobble through the trigger pull. Granted, you can do the same with open sights, but slight movements are not nearly so obvious to the eye.

I also found that, while watching other shooters live-fire, I could watch the laser beam on target and see exactly what they were doing with their handgun during trigger pull and while trying to recover from recoil.

Two additional observations need mention here. If you're working through dry-fire practice with a laser, the laser beam should be adjusted so it appears on target about two inches above your point of aim. Aim with the sights, but watch the laser with your peripheral vision. If you jerk the trigger, the laser will jerk and you will see it. If you are conducting live-fire drills and are having someone coach or watch you, adjust the laser so that it appears on the target below the point you are aiming at with the sights. This way you can concentrate on the sights while your coach watches the laser.

Furthermore, you can dry-fire practice with the laser as the primary sight. Point it at the target and work through the trigger press while not allowing the laser to move. Alternately, you can move the handgun (laser) on the target until it crosses the desired point of aim and pull the trigger at that point, hopefully without making the laser jerk. This is a very good way to learn your handgun's trigger.

When you are considering the time it takes to deploy a handgun from the holster, you may question the speed with which a laser-equipped shooter can turn his laser on before engaging the target. This topic was addressed in the last chapter, and it should be obvious the instinctive activation offered by the Crimson Trace laser grips and Laser Guard are the fastest. But let me add something else here that is often overlooked when it comes to laser-equipped handguns: learning the draw stroke.

Many find it difficult to master getting a handgun out of the holster and orientated towards the target smoothly and efficiently. By watching the laser beam as you draw—with the Crimson Trace products, the laser is activated as soon as you establish your shooting grip around the gun in the holster—you can track muzzle orientation without watching what your hand is doing.

Just the same, new shooters often wonder what makes a good shooting grip. With the Crimson Trace laser grip, it's hard to activate the laser with a bad shooting grip. For most folks, if your grip is activating the laser, then it is a good shooting grip.

So, if the only real advantage of the laser is dry-fire practice and a bit faster and more accurate hip shooting, why spend your money on one? If you have never pulled a gun on someone or held someone at gunpoint, it may be a little hard to understand.

Cops routinely have to take suspects into custody at gunpoint but never pull a trigger. Sometimes these arrests or otherwise serious situations occur in crowds and in the presence of more than one suspect or possible assailant. This type of scenario is very difficult to replicate with any training other than with the use of Simunition (aka high-tech paintball ammunition). The officer must stay focused on the subject he is pointing the pistol at and, at the same time, be cognizant of any other threats that may arise near him and from a variety of directions. The laser allows the officer to do so without any concentration on the sights and makes it much easier for him to be aware of what is developing around him. (RULE No. 8)

Not only that, when you point a handgun at someone and line up the sights for a center mass shot, the handgun covers your view of their danger area, their hands and their waistband where weapons are commonly carried. With a laser sight, you can move your handgun to a high ready, low ready, or even the retention (close ready) position so that you can see your entire assailant and still know—by looking at the red dot on their chest—you have a center mass point of aim.

To further illustrate how important this is, take your carry gun and point it at arm's length in a safe direction while lining up the sights on a point of aim. Now, stand there and hold this position and point of aim for 15 minutes. I bet you can't do it, because your arms will get too tired. Why would you hold a gun on someone for 15 minutes? Well, it may be 15 minutes before the police arrive. With a laser-sighted handgun, you can hold a bad guy at gunpoint until the cows come home. Just drop your arm to your waist and rest your elbow there.

This is significant, because it allows you to keep the weapon close to your body, where you have much more control over it and can secure it more easily. If the troll in your sights decides he wants your gun, or if you are assaulted from another direction by a zombie, vampire, or werewolf, close to your body is where your handgun should be. The beauty of the laser is that if you don't want to, you do not even have to turn it on until you are in the "at gun point" situation.

Are lasers really bright enough to see in any light? Yes and no. In the brightest light, a laser can be hard to see on some surfaces as close as three yards. At night, it's not uncommon to be able to see a laser on target as far as 200 yards away. In common indoor and outdoor lighting, you should always be able to see your laser at least out to around 15 yards; on an overcast day much farther. But here's the thing. If at any time you point your handgun and cannot see the laser—day or night, bad guy or target—revert to your handgun's sights immediately!

Some postulate that, when a bad guy sees the little red dot on their chest, they will instantly surrender. Testimonials expressing this phenomenon abound. I've also heard it said the sound of a pump shotgun chambering a round will make even the most venomous fiend run for the woods. I've no faith in either theory, but don't doubt it can happen. I'll also submit that, under certain conditions, an active laser may disclose your position. The prudent gunfighter will keep the laser off or concealed until he is ready for the enemy to know where he is. With the Crimson Trace laser grip, you can easily conceal the laser beam with your trigger finger (if you are right-handed).

There is one other viable reason I discovered a person may consider a laser sight, and it goes against the statement I offered at the outset about a

laser not being a replacement for fixed sights. Age brings with it bad knees, discounts at McDonald's and, worst of all, bad eyesight for many. I know several police officers nearing retirement who struggle to see their front sights. I'm no different, and front sights are foggy for me. For us, the laser can be a true savior, allowing continued recreational shooting pleasure and personal protection without resorting to a scattergun.

The ability to shoot accurately at night or from the hip, to be able to hold a gangbanger at gunpoint until the cavalry arrives, and to be able to enhance your training are all good reasons for a laser on a handgun. But they may not be the best reasons. A life and death encounter is a dynamic, chaotic situation, one that will likely require you to do things you never expected you might have to do and, very likely, have never done before. Two of these are shooting while you are moving, and shooting from unconventional positions.

Shooting on the move is a difficult thing to do accurately. It challenges the secret—sight alignment and trigger control—because your platform is no longer stable. Not all of us are Todd Jarrett; we do not live and breathe the handgun, we do not practice every day. A handgun fitted with a laser sight allows us normal shooters to focus on the target and forget front and rear sights. It lets us move with the handgun held in any position we want so that we can, with our peripheral vision, see where we're going while we are looking at the threat.

I could attempt to wax on and off about how well a laser will improve your ability to shoot when on the move, but I cannot do it justice. It turns a kiss you're not sure is wanted on the other end into one you know your partner is longing for. You have to experience it to appreciate it.

The same can be said for shooting from freaky positions like you might have to in a life and death situation. You might get knocked to your back, might have to shoot out of your car window to your weak side, hell, you might need to shoot behind you. We cannot predict what you will have to do, but we know that, with a laser-equipped handgun, all you will have to do is get the light on the target and pull the trigger.

By now you should be convinced a laser can be an asset to your survival. At the risk of sounding like a Crimson Trace commercial, the addition of Crimson Trace laser grips to your handgun has no negative impact on your ability to use that gun. After all, they all have a master switch that turns them off completely. Like the tire tool in your car trunk, it is there when you need it, and there are many plausible instances when you just might.

Training Lasers

Can lasers truly impact training in a positive manner? Several methods have already been addressed, but in what other ways can they be an asset?

Shooting is part of my job. I shoot some sort of firearm almost every day. On days I don't shoot, I dry-fire practice, because it helps me stay sharp. But dry-fire practice kind of sucks. There's no bang, no recoil, and no hole in the target. It's sort of mind-numbing, because there's not much feedback. Kinda like an expensive dinner, boring conversation, and no loving at the end. Still, ask any professional shooter and they'll tell you dry-fire practice is part of their routine.

Incorporating a constant-on laser is a way to get more feedback, because you can watch your handgun's orientation in relation to your point of aim through trigger manipulation. Laser/dry-fire practice training like this can be accomplished with any laser sight. However, according to some trainers, it's not "tactically intelligent" training. They contend you watch the laser instead of the sights. This is kind of like saying you should not practice on paper targets because they don't scream or fall down when hit. For advanced shooters, maybe they have a point, but I still find myself occasionally using a constant-on laser to aid work with my trigger pull.

Laser training devices that flash when the hammer falls are an alternative. They fit inside the handgun barrel. Even though you can see the laser flash with your peripheral vision, it still pulls your focus from the sights when you should be concentrating on follow through. I think they can still be viable tools, even for advanced tacticians, and I use them frequently when working on fast weapon presentation at close range. All constant-on handgun lasers are great at confirming weapon orientation during the draw stroke (or at any time for that matter).

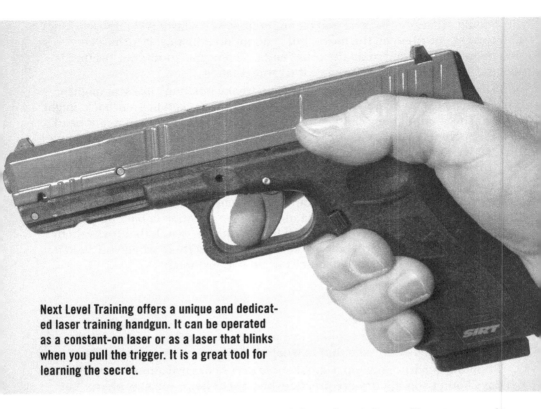

Next Level Training offers a unique and dedicated laser training handgun. It can be operated as a constant-on laser or as a laser that blinks when you pull the trigger. It is a great tool for learning the secret.

Combining a laser training device with LaserLyte's Laser Target seemed to be a great tool to me, especially for mastering the secret, because the target records the impact or flash of the laser for later review. I wanted to find out if, in fact, working with a laser as a training tool could noticeably improve a novice shooter's basic marksmanship skills so I conducted an experiment.

Bat, my son who was 11 at the time of my experiment, has been shooting since he was four. He understands the secret, but is still trying to master it. My wife, Drema, also became more interested in being able to provide for her own protection and security for our kids. I urged her to go to Gunsite, but she wanted some pre-instruction so she wouldn't feel like she was a greenhorn when she got to Arizona. They seemed like perfect research specimens.

I had them both fire three, five-shot groups at three different targets at a distance of seven yards to establish their average group size. For the next five days, they were required to work on the LaserLyte Laser Target using the same handgun and a laser training device.

Both worked with their handguns beyond the mandated 25 trigger pulls for each evening's session. Bat went so far as to conduct his own test, shooting from various positions like he was some sort of covert commando. They actually had fun and appreciated the feedback from the LaserLyte Laser Target.

Five days later, we stepped back out to our Shadowland range. They fired

With the LaserLyte Laser Target, you can actually see your shot group by shoot-ing the display button after several laser shots at the target. You reset the unit by shooting the reset button.

three more five-shot groups. Bat's average group size shrunk by 12 percent, Drema's by 44 percent! Ironically, their initial average group sizes had been identical. Bat demanded another try. After another week of more serious practice using the same minimum, 25 trigger pulls per day routine, he was able to reduce his groups to an average size of 5.08 inches, a 31 percent decrease from his initial attempt.

This experiment reminds me of something Grandpa used to say to us kids: "If you don't know how to shoot, there's no use buying ammunition, 'cause you're just gonna waste it." A laser training device can help you learn the secret without wasting a single round.

A LaserLyte Laser Target and laser trainer will set you back less than the cost of 1,000 rounds of ammunition. The difference is you can practice almost anywhere at almost any time and shoot as much as you want, with no noise, recoil, and muzzle blast distraction.

Fighting Lasers

What should you consider when selecting a laser for a fighting handgun? Let's try to break this down to the nuts and bolts. It needs to be reliable, and we've seen that most are. It also needs to be compatible with how you are going to use it. If you are going to carry concealed, it needs to work with a holster, and the holster needs to be one you can wear comfortably. It also needs to have instant/instinctive activation. In other words, you should be able to activate it by doing nothing more than establishing a shooting grip on your handgun. Beyond that, anything else is mostly personal preference.

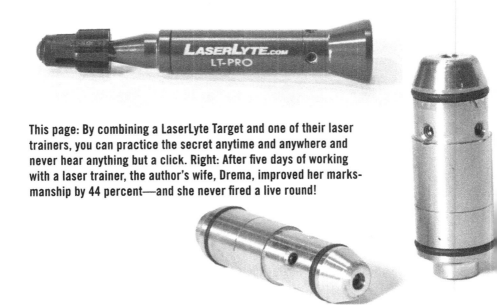

This page: By combining a LaserLyte Target and one of their laser trainers, you can practice the secret anytime and anywhere and never hear anything but a click. Right: After five days of working with a laser trainer, the author's wife, Drema, improved her marksmanship by 44 percent—and she never fired a live round!

With the Laser Ammo SureStrike, you will never wonder if your handgun is unloaded, since the unit is inserted in a handgun's chamber, rendering that gun incapable of chambering a live round.

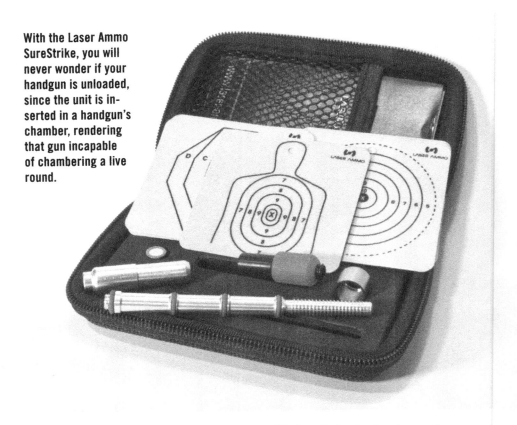

There is something else to consider. We briefly looked at how a laser should be sighted in when conducting basic dry- and live-fire skills practice, depending on the type of practice you're doing. How should it be sighted in if you are conducting more practical live-fire training or when it's being carried on the handgun for personal protection?

For starters, when conducting practical/tactical-type training drills, the laser should be sighted in just as it will when you are carrying it. Opinions vary with regard to where this sight-in is, so let's look at the options and discuss the pros and cons of each. But first, a word or two about laser offset.

Laser offset addresses the fact that the view of the laser on target and the impact of the bullet fired can only exactly coincide at one range. Since the laser is mounted either below, to the side, or both, with regards to the barrel, this point of convergence of the bullet and the laser dot on the target can only be adjusted to coincide at one distance.

What is the best range to establish this crossing of the bullet's path and the laser's beam? It's really not that big a deal inside, say, 20 yards, unless the distance between the center of the bore and the launch point of the laser are drastically different. If you adjust the bullet impact and laser to coincide at, say, 20 yards, there might be an inch or so difference at 10 yards. The key is to ork the coincidence at the longest range possible. This limits the diversion at loser ranges.

The problem is few of us can shoot a good enough group at 50 yards to low precise laser adjustment. I typically adjust lasers on defensive handguns) they will be in line with my point of impact between 10 and 15 yards. This ill generally put the laser to within an inch or so of my bullet impact all the ay out to about 25 yards.

aser Sighting-In Methods

1. Sighted Below Iron Sights—Most who are unfamiliar with lasers and ow they can enhance your ability to hit a target often suggest you sight the ser in so that it cannot be seen if you are using the sights. In other words, the ser is sighted at a point just below the sights. Their thinking is you should ok for the sights first and only transition to the laser if you cannot see the ghts.

I understand their logic; they don't want you looking for a laser that may ot have come on or that might not be very visible for whatever reason. That uld slow down your shooting. For those who intend to only use a laser as backup to iron sights, this would seem to make sense, but, if you are condi- oned to always look over the sights, how will you see the laser without hav- g to take the time to look for it?

2. Sighted on Top of the Front Sight—This is the most common method r sighting in a handgun laser. The laser is adjusted so that it appears right at e top of the front sight on the target. In other words you are kind of capping ur front sight with the laser beam. If you subscribe to the six o'clock hold ethod, this means the laser should indicate the exact point of impact of the llet at one precise distance.

To me, this makes more sense than hiding the laser behind the front sight. t least this way, if your handgun presentation is smooth and you are good at ienting the pistol towards the target, the laser should always be visible. The oblem is this isn't always the case. Even just a slight cant to the handgun, e that still seems to produce a good sight picture, will hide the laser behind e front sight.

3. Sighted Above the Front Sight—This method guarantees the laser will ways be visible. If you present the handgun towards the target and orient correctly, you should always be able to see the laser just above the front ght. This way, if the sights aren't visible, the laser should be and without y head moving or gun canting. It also means you might see a flash sight cture with the laser before you see a flash sight picture with the sights. This much more likely to occur in a chaotic scenario than when on the range, ecause, in a life or death situation, you are more likely to be working off of rget focus.

Think about it this way. You are focusing on the target and presenting the handgun towards the threat. About the time your arms are 60-percent extended, you should be looking for the front sight so you can shift focus or at least obtain a flash sight picture. However, if you are presenting your handgun as you should, it should be oriented at the target long before your arms are 60-percent extended, and with a target focus and supporting light conditions, you should see the laser dot on the target before you could pick up a flash sight picture. Now all you have to do is refine the laser (sight) alignment as you extend your arms and shoot.

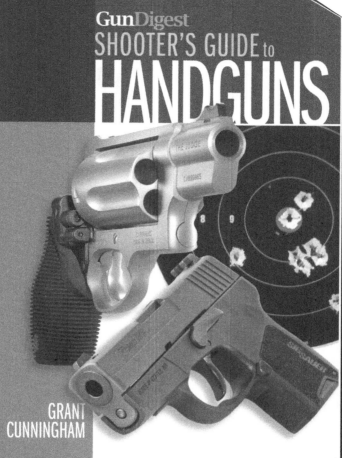

We hope you enjoyed Peter Lessler's *Gun Digest Shooter's Guide to Handgun Marksmanship.* This is just one in the Gun Digest series of *Shooter's Guides,* including:

- *Gun Digest Shooter's Guide to Rifles,* by Wayne van Zwoll
- *Gun Digest Shooter's Guide to Shotguns,* by Terry Wieland
- *Gun Digest Shooter's Guide to Handguns,* by Grant Cunningham

Following is a preview of Grant Cunningham's book.

Please make sure to visit ***www.gundigeststore.com***
to learn more or order any of these excellent books.

WHAT KIND OF HANDGUN DO I NEED?

No matter what you like to shoot, there is a handgun for you. Whether you're interested in hunting, competition, or self defense, you can find a handgun that exactly fits.

Handguns come in three basic styles: single shot, revolver, and autoloader. Each has strengths and weaknesses, and some are better suited to specific activities than others.

THE SINGLE SHOT

The single shot handgun is a staple of hunting and certain kinds of competitive shooting. The single shot has two major attributes: it's generally very strong and able to chamber cartridges that would destroy the typical revolver or autoloader, and it's usually extremely accurate. When you need to place powerful rounds accurately at long distance, the choice is often a single shot.

Single shot handguns were common prior to the invention of the revolver. The classic flintlock, for instance, is (except for a few rare experimental designs) a single shot handgun. The Derringer, the type of gun which famously felled President Lincoln, is typical of a single shot.

Once the revolver was available and economically priced, the single shot rapidly lost favor. It wasn't until the middle of the 20th century, when handgun hunting and long range competition came into vogue, that the single shot made a well-deserved comeback.

Today's single shot handgun is a precision arm that's available in a wide variety of calibers, sighting systems, and barrel lengths - including cartridges that we usually only see in rifles!

BREAK ACTION

The break action is so named because the two parts - the barrel and the frame - are hinged together and opened by "breaking" the gun. (This is very similar to how a double-barrel shotgun works.) Most break action handguns have interchangeable barrels, allowing the shooter to have multiple guns in one.

Break actions are inherently strong guns, and many of them are chambered in rifle cartridges. The Thompson-Center Encore, for instance, can be had in .30-06 and .45-70, among others.

While most break actions are large guns designed for hunting, small break action derringers are made by companies like Bond Arms and American Derringer. These are technically not single shots, as they contain two barrels, but no discussion of break actions would be complete without mentioning them. Available in a range of cartridges, the break action derringers are a popular self defense tool for some people.

ROLLING BLOCK

Although designed by an independent inventor, Leonard Geiger, the rolling block is almost synonymous with the Remington Company due to its adoption of his invention around 1863. Most people think of the rolling block as a rifle action, but Remington's first product utilizing Geiger's action was the Model 1865 pistol.

The rolling block is elegantly simple: the breech block is in the shape of a partial circle, and rotates on a pin. It's locked in by

the similarly-shaped hammer, and can only be opened when the hammer is at full cock. When the hammer drops, it rotates into a depression machined in the breech block, preventing the block from rotating and keeping the cartridge safely contained.

The hammer and breech block are operated almost identically. To load, the hammer is cocked and the breech block thumbed back to open. A round is inserted, and the block is thumbed forward. On firing, the hammer locks the breech closed; once fired, the hammer is cocked again, the breech block is also thumbed open, and the spent cartridge can then be removed.

The rolling block is quite robust, mechanically simple, and very reliable. Today there are only a few rolling block pistols still made, mostly by the Italian reproduction arms companies.

BOLT ACTION

The bolt action pistol is generally regarded as the most accurate, most powerful type of handgun available (though owners of large break-actions like the Thompson/Center Encore might argue the point).

The bolt action pistol operates just like a single shot bolt action rifle. The first commercially successful bolt action pistol was the Remington XP-100, which appeared in 1963. For many years it was the only one of its type available, but in the 1980s and 1990s the growing sport of handgun silhouette (along with increasing interest in handgun hunting) prompted many other companies to make their own version: Weatherby (the CFP), Savage Arms (the Stryker), and Anschutz (the Exemplar), among others, entered the market. Like Remington, however, they discovered that the market was very small, and by 2010 all had been discontinued.

Today there is only one maker of bolt action pistols left, H-S Precision, who make the Pro-Series 2000 line of pistols. However,

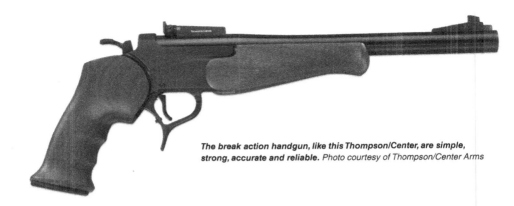

The break action handgun, like this Thompson/Center, are simple, strong, accurate and reliable. Photo courtesy of Thompson/Center Arms

there are many used bolt action pistols on the market in a wide variety of calibers.

ROTATING BREECH

An unusual type of single shot pistol, called the Lone Eagle, was produced by Magnum Research. Long discontinued, it employed a rotating breech block similar to that used in some artillery pieces and was capable of handling powerful rifle calibers. No other handguns of this configuration are currently made.

THE REVOLVER

While the revolver predates the autoloader by decades, it's not at all outdated. The revolver is still made in a wide variety of sizes and calibers, and is still a viable tool for many kinds of shooting, from self defense to hunting.

There are two basic kinds of revolvers: single action and double action. Single-action revolvers are the simplest type: one simply thumbs the hammer back to cock it and pulls the trigger to fire. The term "single" action denotes that the trigger performs only a single task: releasing the sear.

Double actions are so named because the trigger both cocks and releases the hammer. In addition, most double actions can be cocked just like a single action, giving them the best of both worlds: rapid fire by simply pulling the trigger and precise shot placement

by cocking the hammer and taking advantage of the short, light single action trigger.

SINGLE ACTIONS

The single action revolver is the earliest type of repeating handgun, having come into the form we know due to the work of Samuel Colt in 1836. The single action was tough, reliable, and simple to make. These attributes helped it dominate the revolver market in the U.S. well into the 1880s.

The most recognized single action revolver is probably the Colt Model 1873 "Peacemaker," also known as the Single Action Army, or SAA. Even if you've never held one, you've certainly seen them used in westerns on the big screen. This design has undergone only minor changes since it was introduced more than a century ago, and is still made today by Colt. In addition, there are many copies made in Italy as well as the U.S.

Modern single actions, like the Blackhawk from Ruger and the various Freedom Arms revolvers, are very strong and designed to chamber powerful Magnum cartridges. These modern guns are accurate and hard hitting even at a distance, and as a result see the most use in modern handgun hunting and long range competitive shooting.

The reproduction guns, such as the Single Action Army, are most commonly used in the very popular sport of Cowboy Action Shooting. Today it's easy to find high quality copies of the Colt, as well as various Remington and Smith & Wesson models, that fit right into the Old West theme.

DOUBLE ACTIONS

The double action revolver caught on in England long before it was common on these shores. This is slightly ironic, given that England and Europe are generally thought of as being the hotbed of autoloading pistol development.

The double action has changed very little in the last century. In fact, many of the revolver designs on a dealer's shelf are quite similar to those produced in the opening decades of the twentieth century. That isn't to say that there hasn't been progress, however.

Today's revolver is smoother, easier to shoot, and chambers more powerful cartridges than the guns of yesteryear. They're also lighter, often being made of lightweight alloys and polymers. It's possible to buy a Magnum revolver that will fit in a pocket and be scarcely noticeable - in either size or weight. They might not be pleasant to fire because of the fierce recoil, however.

Many double action revolvers are used for personal and home defense, where their ease of shooting and fast reloading - compared to the single action - make them an ideal tool. Because double actions can usually be cocked to single action, they're also used for hunting and long range competitions. It's been said that the double action revolver is the most versatile handgun made, and there is some justification for that belief.

THE AUTOLOADER

According to industry data, well over half of all handguns sold in the U.S. are of the autoloading variety. The autoloading pistol, as its name implies, loads its own chamber after

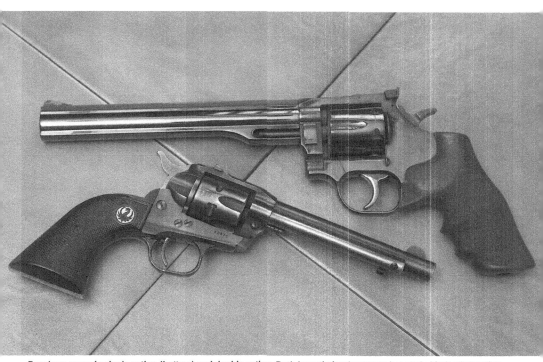

Revolvers come in single action (bottom) and double action. Both have their advantages in certain kinds of shooting.

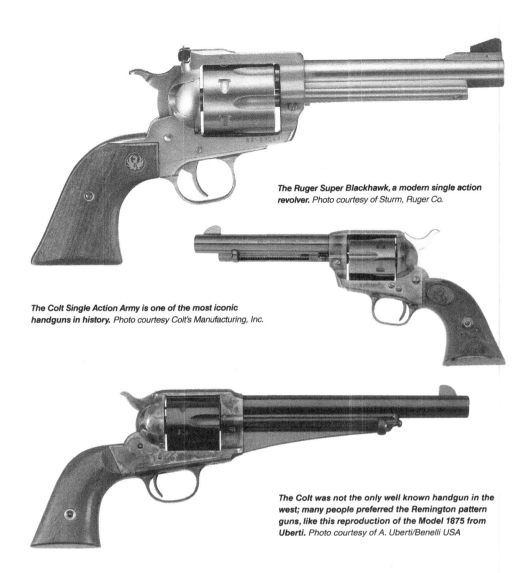

The Ruger Super Blackhawk, a modern single action revolver. Photo courtesy of Sturm, Ruger Co.

The Colt Single Action Army is one of the most iconic handguns in history. Photo courtesy Colt's Manufacturing, Inc.

The Colt was not the only well known handgun in the west; many people preferred the Remington pattern guns, like this reproduction of the Model 1875 from Uberti. Photo courtesy of A. Uberti/Benelli USA

the previous round is fired. It is not fully automatic, as the trigger must be pulled for each round to be fired; they are accurately termed semi-automatic.

Autoloaders, or autos as they're sometimes erroneously called, are available in a wide variety of calibers and a number of different trigger systems. Autoloading pistols are fired by either a hammer, as one might see on a revolver, or by an internal striker as found on a bolt action rifle.

The single action auto, typified by guns like the Model 1911 and the Browning Hi-Power, is much like the single action revolver: the trigger simply releases sear, while the recoiling action of the slide cocks the hammer or striker. Single action autoloaders can have crisp, light triggers that aid in precision marksmanship. Because the gun is usually cocked and ready to fire, single action autoloaders almost always have some sort of safety mechanism that prevents the gun from firing if the trigger is accidentally depressed.

Another type of autoloader is the double/single action, sometimes referred to as "traditional double action" or abbreviated as "DA/SA." The first shot is made with the hammer down; the trigger pulls the hammer back and then releases it, much like the double action revolver.

When the round fires and the slide recoils, it cocks the hammer for the next shot, giving the shooter a lighter single action trigger. Subsequent shots are all done in single action mode. There are also striker-fired autoloaders which operate this way.

The double action auto usually has some sort of mechanism, called a "decocker," to allow the hammer or striker to return to the rest position without firing a round. When the gun is cocked, operating the decocker lowers the hammer or striker without allowing it to contact the round in the chamber. The decocker usually returns to its rest position under spring pressure, but a variant is the combination decocker/safety: it decocks the gun but stays in the activated position, serving to prevent the trigger from functioning. It must be released to be able to fire the gun.

Most decockers are mounted on the slide, but the guns from SIG Sauer are a notable exception. Their decockers are mounted on the side of the frame, just aft of the trigger.

The double action is the most complicated of all autoloaders to use, first because of the differing trigger pulls (the first being long and heavy, and the remaining being short and light), plus the added controls to decock (and possibly on-safe) the gun.

An increasingly popular variant of the double action is called "double action only," usually abbreviated to DAO. The trigger cocks the hammer or striker, releases it, and when the gun recoils the hammer or striker returns to the rest position. The trigger pull is the same all the time: long and heavy, especially compared to a single action gun. Some people call DAO autos "self loading revolvers," because the two have very similar trigger operation.

Most autoloaders are designed with some variation on these three mechanisms, even if not readily apparent. The Glock pistols, for instance, feel to the shooter like they're single action because they have relatively light, short-travel triggers. Technically, though, they're really double action only, because their striker is never fully cocked - it is only pretensioned, and pulling the trigger brings the striker back to the fully cocked position just before it is released.

Autoloaders carry their ammunition in magazines which are inserted into the grip of the gun. Historically this was not the case - there were pistols which loaded with a stripper clip, and those whose magazines were not in the butt - but today all follow the magazine in the grip convention. This makes reloading the autopistol fast and easy.

BLOWBACK, LOCKED BREACH, RECOIL AND GAS OPERATED AUTOS

All autoloaders need a method to keep the brass casing from ejecting before pressures have dropped to a safe level. Having the breech open while still under high pressure could result in serious injury to the shooter.

The simplest method is called "blowback." The breech is held closed by a very strong recoil spring, which slows the movement of the slide just enough for the pressures to drop. This is suited primarily to small, relatively low pressure cartridges and is commonly found on pocket pistols and .22 caliber handguns.

There have been blowback operated guns in calibers like 9mm and .45ACP, but they are not common. The power of their cartridges necessitates extremely strong recoil springs which make their slides difficult to operate. The recoil impulse of a blowback auto is generally more pronounced than that of other mechanisms, making them more difficult to control in rapid shooting. The simplicity of the blowback operation, however, means that the guns are much less expensive to manufacture, which accounts for the low price tags attached to many of them.

The most common form of autoloader operation is the locked breech. There are many different mechanisms to do this, but the concept is simple: the breech is locked in the closed position until the slide has traveled backward a set distance. At that point the pressures have been reduced, and the breech is then allowed to unlock and the empty case is ejected. Because the breech is physically locked and doesn't rely on heavy spring pressure, the slides are usually much easier to operate.

Recoil operated locked breech guns get their motive power from the recoil of the cartridge. The barrel and slide are locked together and the recoil impulse of the round shoves them both backward. After traveling a certain distance, the barrel stops, unlocks from the slide, and allows the slide to continue rearward. As it does it pulls the empty case out of the chamber and throws (ejects) it from the gun. When it hits its rearward travel and starts forward again it strips a new round from the magazine, pushes it into the chamber, and the slide and barrel lock themselves together and travel into their forward rest, or "battery," position - ready for the next shot.

Gas operated autoloaders are much less common. Their breech stays in the lock position as the bullet travels down the barrel;

Striker-fired pistol (top) uses a spring-powered internal firing pin, as contrasted with the hammer-actuated firing pin of pistol below.

The trigger of the single action autoloader is crisp, light, and easy to shoot.

when the bullet reaches a certain point it passes a small hole (or port) which directs a portion of the propellant gas back to the bolt, where it is used to push the slide into an unlocked position. As the slide moves back it behaves much like the recoil operated mechanism, ejecting the old round and, on the return trip, picking up a new round and going back into the battery position.

There have been many variations on these systems over the years. One is the gas delay system, most famously used on the H&K P7 pistol (among others.) The gun is essentially a blowback pistol, but in addition to spring pressure it uses some of the gases to hold the breech close. When the round fires, some of the gas is immediately ported into a small chamber containing a piston which is firmly attached to the slide. The pressure in the chamber delays the piston from being forced back into the chamber, thus delaying the opening of the breech.

The goal of all these mechanisms is the same: to make the gun safe to use. In that sense they all work, but as with any mechanical device they all have their advantages and disadvantages.

AUTOLOADING PISTOL SEQUENCE OF OPERATION

The autopistol is loaded by inserting a magazine into the grip. The slide (or bolt, in some .22 LR pistols) is pulled to the rear and released. As the slide goes forward, it contacts the top round in the magazine and pushes it forward; as the round is pushed, it slides up and into the chamber. The slide then closes on the round.

A single action or traditional double action gun will now be cocked and ready to fire. A DAO-style auto will have the hammer (or striker) in the rest position, ready to by cocked by the trigger. If the gun isn't to be fired immediately, the safety must be engaged or the hammer/striker must be decocked.

To fire, the safety (if any) is released and the trigger pulled. On a single action auto, this releases the hammer or striker to fly forward and ignite the round in the gun. On a double action or DAO gun, the trigger moves the hammer or striker against the mainspring's tension to the fully cocked position, then releases it to fire.

The firing pin/striker hits the primer, which ignites and sets off the powder charge.

The gunpowder burns extremely rapidly and liberates a large amount of very hot gas. This gas very quickly builds to high pressure and forces the bullet out of the case and into the barrel. The gases continue to expand, driving the bullet forward and out of the barrel.

The gun's slide (or bolt) is driven backwards by one of the mechanisms discussed previously. As it starts to move back the barrel unlocks from the slide, usually by dropping down, allowing the slide to continue backward.

As the slide moves to the rear, it pulls (extracts) the empty case from the chamber and ejects it from the gun. As the slide travels back it pushes the hammer (if the gun has one) down and back, cocking it. When the slide hits its rearward travel it stops and then starts forward, pushing the top round in the magazine ahead of it.

As the slide comes back into battery position, it pushes the round fully into the chamber and, if a locked breech design, locks the barrel and slide together. Striker fired guns are usually pre-tensioned at this point as the striker catches on the trigger's sear. The gun is now ready to fire.

DOUBLE ACTION REVOLVER SEQUENCE OF OPERATION

Once the cylinder has been loaded and closed, the pulling of the trigger does several things simultaneously. First, it unlocks the cylinder so that it is free to rotate to a loaded chamber. Once the cylinder is unlocked, a part usually referred to as a "hand" is pushed out of the frame and into contact with the lobes on the extractor star. The hand causes the cylinder to rotate. As all this is happening, the hammer is being cocked against the pressure of the mainspring.

As the trigger continues back, the cylinder continues to rotate until the fresh round is in the position where it aligns with the barrel. Just as it gets there, a small piece of metal (called a bolt or catch) pops into one of the

locking notches on the outside of the cylinder, locking the cylinder into proper alignment with the barrel. The trigger usually continues a very small distance and finally allows the hammer to drop, igniting the round.

When the shooter releases the trigger after firing, it travels forward and resets the hand, cylinder bolt, hammer, and any internal safeties - ready for the next cycle.

(The Smith & Wesson Bodyguard uses a different method of rotating the cylinder, but the sequence is the same.)

THE PERENNIAL QUESTION: REVOLVER OR AUTOLOADER?

Both have their vocal adherents, and both have advantages and disadvantages.

The most commonly cited attribute of the revolver is its inherent reliability. While any mechanical device can malfunction, revolvers have historically had a much longer interval between malfunctions than the autoloader. The revolver also has a simpler manual of arms; there are fewer controls and the gun is more easily reloaded and checked than is the autoloader. The revolver handles ultra-powerful rounds that an autoloader simply can't, making it far more suitable for hunting and long range competition.

The autoloader typically holds more ammunition than does the revolver, and it's generally easier to shoot than a double-action revolver.

Given equal practice most people can reload the autoloader faster than any other handgun, and the autoloader is easier to shoot quickly due to the typically shorter trigger travel. Its ammunition supply is carried in flat, easily-exchanged magazines and the gun itself is flatter - making it, in some opinions, easier to conceal.

How to decide between the two? Start with the expected use. There are some areas where the revolver is going to be the choice: handgun hunting and long-range competitions are areas where autoloaders struggle to

Double action autoloaders need a method to "de-cock" the gun. This Smith & Wesson has decocker on the slide, which also functions as a safety.

The Glock pistols feel much like single actions, but aren't fully cocked until trigger is pulled.

keep up. For self defense, a majority of people prefer an autoloader, but there is a strong contingent of people who make the revolver their choice in protection. In competitive shooting matches some are revolver neutral, where others clearly favor the auto.

The dedication of the shooter is a big determinant as well. The double action revolver is harder to shoot well than the autoloader and demands a greater practice commitment on the part of the shooter. The autoloader, in contrast, is often easier to shoot but has a more difficult manual of arms; it requires more knowledge and care in handling and doing administrative tasks like loading, unloading, and cleaning.

Sometimes physical needs come into play. The autoloaders will generally have a fatter grip than the revolver, making it harder to handle by shooters with shorter fingers or smaller hands. The revolver can be more easily modified for smaller or larger hand sizes simply by changing the grips. Some autoloaders have interchangeable grip parts, but overall still don't have the adjustability of the revolver.

The autoloader's slide can be harder to manipulate for those with muscular issues, while the revolver's cylinder is easy to open and close. Similarly, the revolver's heavy double action trigger requires more finger strength than does the typical autoloader. For someone whose hands are a little on the weak side, the revolver presents a greater challenge than the auto.

One deciding factor is that the auto's slide manipulation is more a matter of technique than strength, but there is no corresponding solution for the person who can't pull the revolver's long and heavy trigger. (In the chapter on shooting techniques, we'll go over the procedure that allows almost anyone to operate almost any autoloader slide, regardless of upper body strength.) In most such cases the autoloader is the better choice.

Of course, for the person who is still having trouble deciding, there is an alternative: buy both!

GETTING THE RIGHT FIT

Shooting a handgun well is greatly helped by proper hand fit. So important is hand fit that some types of competition handguns have grips that are actually molded to the owner's hand. While it's not necessary to go to that extreme for most purposes, making sure that the gun is sized correctly for the hand using it will make it much easier to get good, consistent hits.

To determine whether a given gun and hand are compatible, first make sure that the gun is unloaded; if there is someone else present, have them double-check and verify that it is unloaded. For an autoloader, lock the slide in the open position; for a revolver, leave the cylinder open; for a single shot handgun, leave the bolt or break action open.

Start by placing the finger in the proper position on the trigger. For a single action trigger, the pad of the finger should be centered on the trigger face; for a double action trigger (or any trigger with a pull weight in excess of six pounds or so), it's best to put the crease of the first joint on the face of the trigger for best leverage.

With the trigger finger in place, wrap the rest of the hand around the grip and see which direction the barrel is pointing relative to the bones of the arm. If it's pointing away from the centerline of the forearm, the gun is too large for the hand; if pointing toward the centerline, the gun is too small.

A too-small gun is much easier to deal with than one which is too large. With care it can usually be shot well as-is, and it may be possible to take up the extra space with larger grips. It's the opposite situation - when the gun is too big for the hand - which causes problems.

A too-large gun presents two issues. First, the recoil of the gun will be directed not to-ward the palm, where it is easily absorbed by the hand and the forearm, but against the thumb. The further out on the thumb the recoil is directed, the more painful it will be and the less control the shooter will have over recoil.

Second, the trigger finger will not be able to press the trigger straight to the rear; it will almost always be pushed sideways, causing the muzzle of the gun to drift and the shots to hit to the side of the desired point of aim. This is referred to as "steering the gun," and it's a common cause of poor shooting. While the experienced shooter can compensate for the effect by watching the sights and adjusting where the gun is pointed as the trigger finger moves, the results are never optimal. It's best to have a gun which fits correctly from the start.

Revolvers and most single shot handguns can have smaller grips installed on the gun, and that often results in dramatic changes to the sizing of the gun. Some autoloaders have replaceable grips, though their sizing is not as flexible as with the revolvers and single shots. Some of the newest autoloading pistols have backstraps that are user-replaceable, and they can be a superb solution to fit issues both large and small.

GunDigest
WE KNOW GUNS SO YOU KNOW GUNS
THE MAGAZINE
ENTER TO WIN
NEW PRIZES BEING ADDED ALL THE TIME!
FEDERAL PREMIUM
GOLD MEDAL
HIGH CALIBER
SWEEPSTAKES
www.GunDigest.com
ENTER ONLINE TO WIN! CHECK BACK OFTEN!
NO PURCHASE NECESSARY TO ENTER OR WIN
Open only to legal residents of the United States and the District of Columbia age 18 years or older.
However, because of state regulations, this sweepstakes is not open to residents of Rhode Island.
All fi rearm transfers will be conducted in strict compliance with all applicable federal, state and local laws.
Limit: One online entry per person.